Government Jobs

Or

Private Jobs

Or

Business

for Long-Term Prosperity

Are you tired of the financial treadmill and yearn for lasting financial freedom? In "Financial Freedom Blueprint," embark on a journey that explores the paths of Government Jobs, Private Jobs, and Business, unraveling the secrets to securing a prosperous future for yourself and generations to come.

Discover the keys to unlocking the doors of economic stability and learn how to make the right choices that align with your long-term goals. This book is not just about jobs or business—it's a roadmap to financial emancipation.

Unveiling the Chapters:

Introduction:

In a world where financial stability is a constant pursuit, "Financial Freedom Blueprint" is your compass to navigate the intricate paths of career choices—be it a Government Job, Private Job, or Entrepreneurship. This comprehensive guide goes beyond the surface, delving into the nuances that will shape your financial destiny.

Chapter 1: The Quest for Financial Freedom

In the vast landscape of our aspirations, there exists a singular pursuit that binds us all: the Quest for Financial Freedom. This chapter embarks on a profound exploration into the very essence of this journey—a journey that transcends the mere accumulation of wealth and touches the core of our desires for autonomy, security, and a life well-lived.

Unveiling the Desire:

At the heart of the human experience lies an innate longing for freedom—a desire to break free from the shackles of financial constraints that often dictate the course of our lives. The quest begins with the acknowledgment that financial freedom is not merely about amassing wealth but about gaining control over our destinies.

Section 1: Defining Financial Freedom

Financial freedom is a multifaceted concept, encompassing not only the ability to meet our material needs but also the freedom to pursue our passions, invest in personal growth, and contribute meaningfully to the world. It is about living life on our terms, unburdened by the constant worry of financial instability.

Subsection 1.1: Beyond Monetary Wealth

The quest transcends the mere accumulation of monetary wealth. It involves cultivating a mindset that values experiences over possessions, relationships over transactions, and well-being over opulence. As we navigate the chapters ahead, the narrative unfolds, revealing that financial freedom is a holistic endeavor, touching every aspect of our lives.

Subsection 1.2: Autonomy and Choice
Central to the quest is the attainment of autonomy—the ability to make choices that align with our values and aspirations. Financial freedom empowers individuals to shape their destinies, pursue meaningful careers, and contribute to causes that resonate with their beliefs. The pursuit of autonomy becomes a cornerstone of the journey.

Section 2: The Impact of Financial Freedom

As we delve deeper, it becomes evident that the quest for financial freedom extends beyond personal fulfillment; it has a ripple effect on families, communities, and society at large.

Subsection 2.1: Empowering Generations
One of the profound impacts of financial freedom is its ability to transcend generations. Through strategic planning and wise decision-making, individuals can create a legacy of prosperity that extends far beyond their lifetime. The ability to provide opportunities for the next generation becomes a driving force in the pursuit of financial freedom.

Subsection 2.2: Contributing to Society
Financially liberated individuals are better positioned to contribute to the betterment of society. Whether through philanthropy, community initiatives, or sustainable business practices, the quest for financial freedom becomes a force for positive change, creating a ripple effect that extends far beyond personal gain.

Navigating the Financial Landscape:

The journey unfolds against the backdrop of a dynamic financial landscape—a landscape that offers diverse avenues for wealth creation and financial stability. In the chapters to come, we will explore these avenues, dissecting the nuances of government jobs, private jobs, entrepreneurship, and various investment strategies.

Section 3: Understanding Financial Avenues

Subsection 3.1: Government Jobs - Stability and Service

Government jobs emerge as a foundational pillar of financial stability. We explore the merits of a career in public service, the security it provides, and the avenues for personal and professional growth within the bureaucratic framework.

Subsection 3.2: Private Jobs - Corporate Ascent

Private jobs, with their dynamic environments and opportunities for rapid advancement, take center stage. We unravel the intricacies of climbing the corporate ladder, navigating office politics, and leveraging private sector opportunities for financial gain.

Subsection 3.3: Entrepreneurship - Risk and Reward

Entrepreneurship, the frontier of innovation and risk-taking, becomes a focal point. We delve into the art of building businesses, exploring case studies of those who have achieved financial freedom through entrepreneurship, and dissecting the challenges and triumphs that come with being one's own boss.

Section 4: Navigational Tools

Subsection 4.1: Education as a Catalyst

Education emerges as a powerful catalyst in the pursuit of financial freedom. From formal degrees to continuous learning, we unravel the transformative impact of education in shaping careers, enhancing skills, and opening doors to new opportunities.

Subsection 4.2: Skills for Tomorrow

Building on the educational foundation, we explore the importance of acquiring and honing skills that are in high demand. In a world shaped by rapid technological advancements, staying relevant and adaptable becomes a key aspect of securing financial stability.

The Psychological Landscape:

Beyond the tangible aspects of wealth creation and career choices, the quest for financial freedom delves into the psychological landscape of aspirations, fears, and mindset shifts.

Section 5: The Psychology of Financial Freedom

Subsection 5.1: Unraveling Aspirations
The pursuit of financial freedom often begins with unearthing and understanding personal aspirations. We delve into the process of identifying goals, both short-term and long-term, and how aligning one's financial journey with these aspirations becomes a catalyst for success.

Subsection 5.2: Overcoming Financial Fears
Simultaneously, the journey involves confronting and overcoming financial fears. Whether it's the fear of failure, the fear of taking calculated risks, or the fear of scarcity, we explore strategies to navigate these fears and turn them into stepping stones toward financial freedom.

The Quest Unfolds:

As this inaugural chapter unfolds, it lays the groundwork for the extensive exploration ahead. The quest for financial freedom, multifaceted and deeply personal, becomes a narrative that extends beyond the pages of this book. It is a journey of self-discovery, strategic decision-making, and a commitment to a life of autonomy, impact, and lasting prosperity.

As we turn the pages and venture into the subsequent chapters, each facet of the quest will be meticulously unveiled. The path to financial freedom awaits, and the expedition has only just begun.

Chapter 2: The Government Job Dilemma: Stability vs. Growth

In the intricate web of career choices, the allure of government jobs beckons individuals with promises of stability, security, and a well-defined career path. Yet, as we embark on an in-depth exploration in this chapter, the dichotomy between stability and growth emerges as a central theme—a dilemma that many individuals grapple with when deciding on their professional trajectory.

Understanding the Appeal:

Section 1: The Allure of Stability

Subsection 1.1: Job Security in Government Roles
Government jobs are often synonymous with job security. The stability they offer, particularly in times of economic uncertainty, becomes a compelling factor for individuals seeking a reliable source of income. The prospect of a steady paycheck, benefits, and a pension plan creates a sense of financial assurance that resonates with many.

Subsection 1.2: Defined Career Trajectory

A government career typically follows a well-defined trajectory. With clear hierarchies, promotions based on tenure and performance, and predetermined salary scales, individuals entering government service can anticipate the progression of their careers. This structured path appeals to those who value predictability in their professional lives.

Section 2: Navigating the Bureaucratic Landscape

Subsection 2.1: Bureaucratic Stability

The bureaucratic stability inherent in government jobs can provide a sense of order and structure. Policies, procedures, and regulations guide decision-making, contributing to an environment where individuals know what to expect. This predictability is often perceived as an asset, fostering a work atmosphere that thrives on consistency.

Subsection 2.2: Pension and Retirement Benefits

Government jobs frequently come with pension plans and retirement benefits, offering a long-term financial safety net. This aspect becomes increasingly significant as individuals consider their future and the desire for financial security during retirement. The assurance of a pension adds a layer of financial stability that is not always guaranteed in the private sector.

The Trade-Off: Stability vs. Growth

Section 3: The Limitations of Stability

Subsection 3.1: Bureaucratic Rigidity

While stability is a cornerstone of government jobs, it comes with its own set of limitations. Bureaucratic rigidity can stifle innovation and impede quick decision-making. The hierarchical nature of government organizations may result in bureaucratic red tape, making it challenging for individuals to implement fresh ideas or respond swiftly to changing circumstances.

Subsection 3.2: Limited Financial Upside

While the stability of a government job provides financial security, it often comes at the cost of limited financial upside. Salary increases may be predetermined, and the potential for significant income growth is constrained compared to the potentially lucrative opportunities available in the private sector.

Section 4: The Urge for Professional Growth

Subsection 4.1: Ambitions Beyond Stability

Many individuals, despite valuing stability, harbor ambitions beyond the confines of a predictable career trajectory. The desire for professional growth, challenging assignments, and the opportunity to make a broader impact can become powerful motivators that challenge the allure of stability.

Subsection 4.2: The Glass Ceiling of Government Roles

Government jobs, though stable, can be accompanied by a perceived glass ceiling. Advancement may be based on seniority rather than merit, and achieving higher positions can be a prolonged process. This limitation prompts ambitious individuals to explore alternative paths that offer a faster ascent up the career ladder.

Strategies for Navigating the Dilemma:

Section 5: Balancing Stability and Growth

Subsection 5.1: Strategic Career Planning

Individuals facing the government job dilemma can benefit from strategic career planning. This involves aligning personal and professional goals with the inherent characteristics of government roles. Identifying opportunities for growth within the bureaucratic framework becomes crucial for those seeking a balance between stability and advancement.

Subsection 5.2: Leveraging Training and Development Programs

Government organizations often provide training and development programs. Individuals can proactively engage in these initiatives to enhance their skills, making themselves more valuable to their departments. This not only contributes to personal growth but can also position them for promotions and increased responsibilities.

Section 6: Exploring Hybrid Career Paths

Subsection 6.1: Combining Government Service with External Ventures
Ambitious individuals may choose to explore hybrid career paths, combining the stability of a government job with external ventures. This could involve pursuing entrepreneurial endeavors, consulting roles, or engaging in side projects that provide an additional avenue for professional growth and financial rewards.

Subsection 6.2: Networking Beyond Government Circles
Networking plays a pivotal role in career growth. Individuals contemplating a government career can benefit from expanding their professional network beyond bureaucratic circles. Engaging with professionals from diverse sectors can open doors to opportunities, mentorship, and insights that may not be readily available within the confines of government offices.

Case Studies: Balancing Stability and Ambition

Section 7: Real-Life Narratives

Subsection 7.1: The Career Trajectory of [Name]
Explore the journey of [Name], an individual who navigated the government job dilemma by strategically leveraging training programs, networking, and pursuing external ventures. [Name]'s story serves as a testament to the possibilities of achieving both stability and growth within the realm of government service.

Subsection 7.2: Lessons from [Another Name]
Learn from the experiences of [Another Name], who chose a hybrid career path, combining a government role with entrepreneurial pursuits. [Another Name]'s narrative sheds light on the

challenges and triumphs of navigating the government job dilemma while actively seeking professional growth beyond bureaucratic boundaries.

The Path Forward:

Section 8: Crafting Your Unique Journey

Subsection 8.1: Self-Reflection and Goal Setting
Individuals contemplating or currently engaged in government service are encouraged to embark on a journey of self-reflection. Define personal and professional goals, considering both the desire for stability and the urge for growth. Goal setting becomes the compass guiding individuals through the complexities of the government job dilemma.

Subsection 8.2: Embracing a Dynamic Perspective
Recognize that the government job dilemma is not a binary choice but a dynamic spectrum. Embrace a perspective that allows for fluidity in career decisions. Individuals can oscillate between periods of prioritizing stability and phases of actively pursuing growth, crafting a career journey that evolves with their aspirations.

Conclusion:

As we navigate the government job dilemma, it becomes evident that the choice between stability and growth is not a one-size-fits-all decision. The intricate interplay of personal values, career ambitions, and the nuances of the bureaucratic landscape requires individuals to chart their unique paths.

The journey is not defined solely by the career chosen but by the intentional decisions made along the way. In the subsequent chapters, we will continue our exploration, unraveling the complexities of private jobs, entrepreneurship, and the multifaceted landscape of financial freedom. The dichotomy between stability and growth is just one facet of the broader quest for a life of prosperity and fulfillment.

Chapter 3: Private Jobs - Climbing the Corporate Ladder to Prosperity

In the realm of private jobs, a dynamic and competitive landscape unfolds. This chapter embarks on a comprehensive exploration of the intricacies involved in climbing the corporate ladder to prosperity. Private jobs offer a tapestry of opportunities, challenges, and rewards, making this journey a fascinating and often complex pursuit for individuals seeking financial success and professional growth.

Navigating the Corporate Landscape:

Section 1: The Allure of Private Jobs

Subsection 1.1: Dynamic Work Environments
Private jobs are renowned for their dynamic work environments. Unlike the bureaucratic structures of government roles, the private sector thrives on adaptability, innovation, and a constant pursuit of excellence. This dynamic nature appeals to individuals seeking a fast-paced and ever-evolving professional journey.

Subsection 1.2: Merit-Based Advancement

In private jobs, career progression is often tied to merit and performance. Individuals who contribute significantly to the success of their organizations are frequently rewarded with opportunities for advancement. This merit-based system encourages a culture of ambition and excellence, fueling the climb up the corporate ladder.

Section 2: The Corporate Ascent

Subsection 2.1: Climbing Through the Ranks

Climbing the corporate ladder is a journey marked by ascending through the ranks of an organization. From entry-level positions to executive roles, individuals navigate a hierarchy where each rung represents new challenges, responsibilities, and, ideally, increased financial rewards.

Subsection 2.2: Specialization and Expertise

Specialization and expertise become valuable assets in the corporate world. Individuals who cultivate specialized skills in their respective fields often find themselves in high demand. This expertise not only contributes to professional growth but also enhances the individual's ability to command a competitive salary.

The Trade-Off: Challenges Amid Prosperity

Section 3: The Challenges of Private Employment

Subsection 3.1: Work-Life Balance Struggles

While the dynamic nature of private jobs can be invigorating, it often comes at the cost of work-life balance. The pressure to meet ambitious targets, tight deadlines, and the constant pursuit of professional growth can lead to challenges in maintaining a healthy equilibrium between work and personal life.

Subsection 3.2: Job Insecurity in a Competitive Environment

In the pursuit of prosperity, individuals in private jobs may face the specter of job insecurity. The competitive nature of the private sector means that organizations must adapt rapidly to market changes. This adaptability sometimes translates to restructuring, downsizing, or even job insecurity for employees.

Section 4: Strategies for Corporate Success

Subsection 4.1: Skill Development and Continuous Learning
In the corporate world, success often hinges on the ability to adapt and acquire new skills. Continuous learning becomes a cornerstone for individuals aiming to climb the corporate ladder. From leadership training to staying abreast of industry trends, investing in one's skill set becomes a strategic move for long-term success.

Subsection 4.2: Building a Professional Network
Networking plays a pivotal role in corporate success. Building and nurturing a professional network opens doors to mentorship, career opportunities, and valuable insights. Individuals who actively cultivate relationships within and beyond their organizations often find themselves better positioned for advancement.

Section 5: Balancing Ambition and Well-Being

Subsection 5.1: Setting Realistic Career Goals
While ambition is a driving force in climbing the corporate ladder, setting realistic career goals is paramount. Individuals must align their aspirations with the opportunities and challenges presented by their chosen industries. Setting achievable milestones ensures a sense of accomplishment and guards against burnout.

Subsection 5.2: Prioritizing Mental and Physical Health
Maintaining well-being amidst corporate demands is a crucial consideration. Individuals climbing the ladder must prioritize mental and physical health to sustain their energy, focus, and resilience.

Strategies such as mindfulness, exercise, and a healthy work-life balance contribute to overall well-being.

The Corporate Culture:

Section 6: Corporate Culture and Values

Subsection 6.1: Aligning with Organizational Values
Corporate culture plays a significant role in an individual's journey through private employment. Aligning personal values with the values of the organization fosters a sense of purpose and belonging. Individuals who resonate with their company's ethos often find greater satisfaction and success in their roles.

Subsection 6.2: Navigating Office Politics
Office politics is an inherent aspect of corporate life. Navigating these dynamics requires emotional intelligence, tact, and effective communication. Individuals who understand and navigate office politics strategically can build alliances, influence decision-making, and enhance their prospects for success.

Case Studies: Personal Narratives of Corporate Ascent

Section 7: Real-Life Stories

Subsection 7.1: The Corporate Odyssey of [Name]
Explore the corporate ascent of [Name], an individual who navigated the challenges of private employment to achieve executive leadership. [Name]'s story serves as an inspiration, shedding light on the strategic decisions, resilience, and continuous learning that propelled them up the corporate ladder.

Subsection 7.2: Lessons from [Another Name]

Learn from the experiences of [Another Name], who successfully balanced ambition with well-being throughout their corporate journey. [Another Name]'s narrative provides insights into the importance of networking, skill development, and maintaining a healthy work-life balance.

The Path Forward:

Section 8: Shaping Your Corporate Journey

Subsection 8.1: Crafting a Long-Term Career Strategy
Individuals navigating private employment are encouraged to craft a long-term career strategy. This involves setting clear goals, investing in skill development, and actively managing one's professional network. A strategic approach ensures sustained success and resilience in the face of challenges.

Subsection 8.2: Embracing the Journey with Purpose
Amidst the complexities of corporate ascent, individuals are reminded to embrace the journey with purpose. Success is not solely measured by the title or salary but by the fulfillment derived from meaningful work, personal growth, and contributions to the organization and community.

Conclusion:

As we conclude this exploration into private jobs and the climb up the corporate ladder, it becomes evident that the journey is as nuanced as the individuals undertaking it. The allure of prosperity is tempered by the challenges and trade-offs inherent in private employment. Yet, with strategic planning, continuous learning, and a focus on well-being, individuals can chart a path to success and fulfillment in the dynamic world of private jobs.

In the upcoming chapters, we will delve further into the entrepreneurial landscape and the multifaceted choices individuals face on the quest for lasting financial freedom. The corporate ladder is just one avenue, and the exploration continues as we unravel the complexities of career choices and financial success.

Chapter 4: Entrepreneurship - The Business of Building Wealth

Entrepreneurship, a venture into the unknown, is a journey laden with risks, rewards, and the promise of financial freedom. In this chapter, we embark on a comprehensive exploration of the world of entrepreneurship—a realm where individuals carve their paths, innovate, and strive to build not just businesses but lasting wealth and prosperity.

Embracing the Entrepreneurial Spirit:

Section 1: The Essence of Entrepreneurship

Subsection 1.1: Defining Entrepreneurship
At its core, entrepreneurship is the art of identifying opportunities, taking calculated risks, and creating value. It involves transforming ideas into tangible products or services that meet market needs. The essence of entrepreneurship lies in the pursuit of innovation, independence, and the potential for significant financial rewards.

Subsection 1.2: The Entrepreneurial Mindset

Entrepreneurship is not merely a profession; it's a mindset. Individuals with an entrepreneurial spirit exhibit traits such as resilience, creativity, adaptability, and a willingness to embrace uncertainty. This mindset forms the foundation for navigating the challenges and seizing the opportunities inherent in the entrepreneurial journey.

Navigating the Entrepreneurial Landscape:

Section 2: The Dynamics of Business Creation

Subsection 2.1: From Idea to Business

The journey of entrepreneurship often begins with an idea—a solution to a problem or an innovative concept. Transforming this idea into a viable business involves market research, feasibility studies, and strategic planning. Entrepreneurs navigate the intricacies of business creation, from conceptualization to the establishment of a tangible and scalable enterprise.

Subsection 2.2: Business Models and Revenue Streams

Entrepreneurs must meticulously design business models that outline how their enterprises will operate and generate revenue. This involves choosing the right revenue streams, pricing strategies, and distribution channels. Crafting a sustainable and profitable business model is a pivotal step in the entrepreneurial journey.

Section 3: Risks and Rewards

Subsection 3.1: Calculated Risks in Entrepreneurship

Risk is inherent in entrepreneurship, but successful entrepreneurs excel in taking calculated risks. This involves assessing potential challenges, understanding market dynamics, and making strategic decisions that maximize opportunities while mitigating risks. The ability to navigate uncertainty becomes a hallmark of entrepreneurial success.

Subsection 3.2: The Rewards of Entrepreneurship

While entrepreneurship entails risks, the potential rewards are equally significant. Entrepreneurs have the opportunity to build wealth through the success of their ventures. Financial rewards, personal fulfillment, and the ability to create a lasting impact on society are among the myriad benefits that await those who embark on the entrepreneurial path.

Building a Successful Business:

Section 4: Strategies for Entrepreneurial Success

Subsection 4.1: Market Research and Validation

Successful entrepreneurs prioritize thorough market research to understand customer needs, identify competitors, and validate their business ideas. This foundational step ensures that their ventures are built on a solid understanding of market dynamics and consumer preferences.

Subsection 4.2: Innovation and Adaptability

Innovation is the lifeblood of entrepreneurship. Entrepreneurs continually seek ways to differentiate their products or services, staying ahead of market trends and meeting evolving consumer demands. The ability to adapt to changing circumstances and embrace innovation is a key determinant of entrepreneurial success.

Section 5: Scaling and Growth

Subsection 5.1: Scaling Strategies

As successful ventures gain traction, entrepreneurs face the challenge of scaling their businesses. This involves expanding operations, reaching new markets, and increasing production capacity. Entrepreneurs must develop scalable strategies that allow their businesses to grow while maintaining efficiency and profitability.

Subsection 5.2: Financial Management

Entrepreneurial success hinges on effective financial management. Entrepreneurs must master budgeting, cash flow management, and strategic financial planning. Sound financial practices ensure the sustainability of the business and lay the groundwork for long-term wealth creation.

The Entrepreneurial Lifestyle:

Section 6: Balancing Passion and Practicality

Subsection 6.1: Pursuing Passionate Ventures

Entrepreneurs often pursue ventures aligned with their passions. This alignment fosters dedication, resilience, and a deep sense of purpose. However, balancing passion with practicality is crucial to ensure that business decisions are grounded in market realities and strategic considerations.

Subsection 6.2: Navigating Lifestyle Changes

The entrepreneurial lifestyle can be demanding, requiring dedication and time investment. Entrepreneurs must navigate lifestyle changes, adapting to the demands of business ownership while maintaining a healthy work-life balance. Strategies for managing stress, prioritizing self-care, and nurturing personal relationships become paramount.

The Impact of Entrepreneurship:

Section 7: Creating Jobs and Economic Impact

Subsection 7.1: Job Creation

Entrepreneurship is a powerful driver of job creation. Successful entrepreneurs not only build wealth for themselves but also contribute to the economic growth of their communities by generating employment opportunities. The ability to create jobs is a social and economic impact that distinguishes entrepreneurs as key contributors to society.

Subsection 7.2: Innovation and Societal Advancement

Entrepreneurs often lead the charge in innovation, driving technological advancements and societal progress. The solutions they create address pressing challenges, improve efficiency, and enhance the quality of life. The impact of entrepreneurship extends beyond individual wealth creation to the betterment of society as a whole.

Case Studies: Tales of Entrepreneurial Triumph

Section 8: Real-Life Narratives

Subsection 8.1: The Entrepreneurial Odyssey of [Name]
Explore the entrepreneurial journey of [Name], a visionary who transformed a creative idea into a thriving business. [Name]'s story serves as an inspiration, shedding light on the strategic decisions, challenges faced, and ultimate triumph that characterize entrepreneurial success.

Subsection 8.2: Lessons from [Another Name]
Learn from the experiences of [Another Name], an entrepreneur who navigated the complexities of scaling a business while maintaining a commitment to sustainable practices. [Another Name]'s narrative provides insights into the challenges and rewards of entrepreneurship with a focus on societal impact.

The Path Forward:

Section 9: Charting Your Entrepreneurial Course

Subsection 9.1: Identifying Opportunities
Individuals contemplating entrepreneurship are encouraged to identify opportunities that align with their passions, skills, and market demands. A keen awareness of potential business niches lays the groundwork for a successful entrepreneurial journey.

Subsection 9.2: Developing an Entrepreneurial Mindset

Embracing an entrepreneurial mindset involves cultivating traits such as resilience, adaptability, and a willingness to take calculated risks. Individuals can actively develop these attributes, fostering the mindset required to navigate the challenges and seize the opportunities of entrepreneurship.

Conclusion:

As we conclude this exploration into entrepreneurship, it becomes evident that the entrepreneurial journey is as diverse as the individuals who embark on it. The pursuit of wealth through business creation is a dynamic and transformative experience—one marked by innovation, resilience, and the potential for lasting impact.

In the forthcoming chapters, we will delve into additional facets

Chapter 5: Weighing the Pros and Cons - Deciding Your Path

In the labyrinth of career choices, the decision between government jobs, private jobs, and entrepreneurship becomes a pivotal crossroad. This chapter serves as a comprehensive guide, delving into the nuanced pros and cons of each path. As individuals stand at the precipice of choice, the goal is to provide clarity, enabling them to make informed decisions aligned with their aspirations for long-term financial freedom.

The Decision-Making Framework:

Section 1: Defining Your Values and Priorities

Subsection 1.1: Identifying Core Values
The decision-making journey begins with a deep exploration of personal values. What matters most to you? Stability, autonomy, innovation, or societal impact? Identifying core values forms the bedrock of a decision-making framework that aligns with your intrinsic motivations.

Subsection 1.2: Prioritizing Long-Term Goals
Consider your long-term goals and aspirations. Are you driven by the desire for financial stability, rapid career growth, or the autonomy to chart your own course? Prioritizing these goals provides a roadmap for evaluating the pros and cons of government jobs, private jobs, and entrepreneurship.

Section 2: Government Jobs - The Stalwart of Stability

Subsection 2.1: The Pros of Government Jobs

Stability and Job Security: Government jobs offer a stable work environment and job security, providing a reliable source of income even during economic uncertainties.
Pension and Benefits: Robust pension plans and comprehensive benefits packages contribute to long-term financial security.
Defined Career Trajectory: Clear hierarchies and predetermined career paths enable individuals to plan their professional growth with certainty.

Subsection 2.2: The Cons of Government Jobs

Bureaucratic Rigidity: The structured nature of government organizations can sometimes stifle innovation and hinder quick decision-making.
Limited Financial Upside: While stable, government jobs may offer limited financial growth compared to the potentially lucrative opportunities in the private sector.

Section 3: Private Jobs - The Dynamic Landscape of Opportunity

Subsection 3.1: The Pros of Private Jobs

Dynamic Work Environments: Private jobs thrive on adaptability, providing a dynamic work environment that appeals to those seeking constant challenges.
Merit-Based Advancement: Career progression is often tied to merit, offering individuals the opportunity for rapid advancement based on performance.
Financial Growth Potential: Private jobs often come with the potential for higher salaries and financial rewards, especially as individuals climb the corporate ladder.

Subsection 3.2: The Cons of Private Jobs

Work-Life Balance Challenges: The dynamic nature of private jobs can lead to challenges in maintaining a healthy work-life balance.
Job Insecurity: The competitive private sector may entail job insecurity, with organizations adapting rapidly to market changes.

Section 4: Entrepreneurship - The Journey of Innovation and Risk

Subsection 4.1: The Pros of Entrepreneurship

Innovation and Creativity: Entrepreneurs have the freedom to innovate, create, and build solutions to address market needs.
Unlimited Financial Potential: The potential for significant financial rewards is a driving force, with entrepreneurs having the ability to build wealth through successful ventures.

Autonomy and Independence: Entrepreneurship provides autonomy and the opportunity to be your own boss, shaping the direction of your ventures.

Subsection 4.2: The Cons of Entrepreneurship

High Level of Risk: Entrepreneurship comes with inherent risks, and ventures may face uncertainty, financial challenges, and even failure.
Workload and Stress: The entrepreneurial journey can be demanding, often requiring extensive time investment and potentially leading to stress and burnout.
Lack of Stability: The stability offered by traditional employment may be absent in entrepreneurial pursuits.

Navigating Your Decision:

Section 5: Case Studies - Realizing the Paths

Subsection 5.1: The Journey of [Name] - Government Job Stalwart

Explore the career journey of [Name], who found fulfillment and stability in a government job.

[Name]'s story illustrates the positive impact of a government career on long-term financial security and job stability.

Subsection 5.2: [Another Name]'s Corporate Odyssey - Private Job Success

Discover the corporate ascent of [Another Name], who navigated the private sector to achieve financial growth and career success. [Another Name]'s narrative showcases the potential rewards of a dynamic private job.

Subsection 5.3: [Yet Another Name]'s Entrepreneurial Triumph

Journey with [Yet Another Name], an entrepreneur who built wealth through innovative ventures. [Yet Another Name]'s story highlights the risks and rewards of entrepreneurship, showcasing the potential for autonomy and financial success.

Section 6: Decision-Making Strategies

Subsection 6.1: Comprehensive Analysis

Conduct a comprehensive analysis of your values, priorities, and long-term goals. Evaluate how each path aligns with your intrinsic motivations and aspirations for financial freedom.

Subsection 6.2: Flexibility and Adaptability

Embrace flexibility and adaptability in your decision-making process. Recognize that career paths are not static, and individuals often transition between government jobs, private jobs, and entrepreneurship at different stages of their lives.

Section 7: Seeking Professional Guidance

Subsection 7.1: Career Counselors and Mentors

Engage with career counselors or mentors who can provide insights, guidance, and mentorship. Their experience and perspective can offer valuable input in shaping your decision-making process.

Subsection 7.2: Networking and Informational Interviews

Expand your professional network and conduct informational interviews with individuals who have pursued government jobs, private jobs, or entrepreneurship. Learning from their experiences can provide valuable insights.

Conclusion:

As you stand at the crossroads of government jobs, private jobs, and entrepreneurship, remember that the decision is not a one-size-fits-all proposition. It's a dynamic choice that evolves with your values, priorities, and goals. By weighing the pros and cons, exploring real-life narratives, and adopting a strategic decision-making approach, you pave the way for a career path that aligns with your vision for long-term financial freedom.

In the chapters that follow, we will delve deeper into specific aspects of each path, providing actionable insights and strategies to empower your journey towards prosperity and fulfillment. The decision is yours to make, and the path forward awaits your deliberate and informed choice.

Chapter 6: Investing in Education - A Gateway to Success

Education is the cornerstone of personal and professional development, serving as a transformative force that opens doors to opportunities, enhances skills, and empowers individuals to navigate the complexities of the modern world. In this chapter, we embark on a comprehensive exploration of the myriad ways in which investing in education serves as a gateway to success, fostering lifelong learning and sustainable growth.

The Transformative Power of Education:

Section 1: The Intrinsic Value of Learning

Subsection 1.1: The Lifelong Learning Paradigm
Education is not confined to the classroom; it is a lifelong journey of acquiring knowledge, skills, and perspectives. Embracing a mindset of lifelong learning positions individuals to adapt to change, seize opportunities, and continually evolve in an ever-shifting landscape.

Subsection 1.2: Beyond Credentials - Skill Development
While degrees and certifications hold value, the true essence of education lies in skill development. Investing in the acquisition and enhancement of skills equips individuals with the tools needed to excel in their chosen fields, fostering a competitive edge in the professional realm.

Section 2: The Economic Impact of Education

Subsection 2.1: Career Advancement and Income Growth

Education serves as a catalyst for career advancement and income growth. Individuals with higher levels of education often command better-paying jobs and have increased access to opportunities for professional development and upward mobility.

Subsection 2.2: Education and Economic Stability

Societal and economic stability are intertwined with the educational attainment of a populace. Investments in education contribute to a skilled workforce, innovation, and the creation of a robust economic ecosystem that benefits individuals and communities.

Navigating Educational Paths:

Section 3: Formal Education - Degrees and Certifications

Subsection 3.1: The Value of Degrees

Higher education degrees, such as bachelor's, master's, and doctoral degrees, provide in-depth knowledge and specialized expertise in specific fields. The attainment of degrees opens doors to a range of career opportunities and signifies a commitment to academic excellence.

Subsection 3.2: Professional Certifications and Skill-Specific Training

In addition to traditional degrees, professional certifications and skill-specific training programs play a pivotal role in enhancing one's skill set. These targeted educational pursuits address the evolving needs of industries, offering a practical and focused approach to skill development.

Section 4: Informal Education - Online Learning and Self-Directed Learning

Subsection 4.1: The Rise of Online Learning

The digital era has ushered in a revolution in education, with online learning platforms offering accessible and flexible opportunities for individuals to acquire new knowledge and skills. Online courses, webinars, and e-learning modules enable self-directed learning at one's own pace.

Subsection 4.2: Self-Directed Learning and Personal Development
Beyond formal courses, self-directed learning empowers individuals to explore diverse topics of interest, cultivate new hobbies, and foster personal development. This intrinsic motivation for learning contributes to a well-rounded and intellectually agile individual.

The Intersection of Education and Career:

Section 5: Education as a Career Catalyst

Subsection 5.1: Aligning Education with Career Goals
Strategic alignment between education and career goals is essential. Individuals benefit from identifying educational paths that not only align with their interests but also equip them with the skills required for success in their chosen careers.

Subsection 5.2: Networking and Mentorship in Educational Pursuits
Networking and mentorship play crucial roles in educational and career journeys. Engaging with educators, industry professionals, and peers fosters a supportive environment that enhances learning outcomes and provides valuable insights into career pathways.

Educational Investments and Returns:

Section 6: Return on Educational Investment

Subsection 6.1: Economic Returns
Investments in education yield economic returns through increased earning potential, career advancement, and access to a broader range of job opportunities. Individuals with higher educational qualifications tend to experience a more favorable return on investment in their careers.

Subsection 6.2: Non-Monetary Returns

Beyond monetary gains, education contributes to non-monetary returns such as personal growth, intellectual fulfillment, and a sense of empowerment. These intangible benefits enhance the overall quality of life and well-being.

Section 7: Scholarships, Grants, and Financial Aid

Subsection 7.1: Access to Educational Opportunities

Scholarships, grants, and financial aid programs play a pivotal role in ensuring equal access to educational opportunities. These resources alleviate financial barriers, enabling individuals from diverse backgrounds to pursue their educational aspirations.

Subsection 7.2: Maximizing Financial Resources

Understanding the landscape of scholarships and financial aid options empowers individuals to maximize available resources. Strategic planning and diligent research enhance the financial feasibility of educational investments.

Lifelong Learning for Personal and Professional Growth:

Section 8: Lifelong Learning as a Career Strategy

Subsection 8.1: Adapting to Changing Industries

In dynamic industries, lifelong learning becomes a strategic career tool. Adapting to emerging trends, technologies, and industry shifts through continuous education positions individuals for relevance and success in their professional journeys.

Subsection 8.2: Skill Stacking and Career Agility

Skill stacking involves combining diverse skills to create a unique and valuable skill set. This approach, coupled with ongoing education, enhances career agility, allowing individuals to navigate various roles and industries throughout their careers.

Case Studies: Educational Journeys to Success

Section 9: Real-Life Narratives

Subsection 9.1: [Name] - From Educational Pursuits to Career Triumph
Explore the educational journey of [Name], an individual who strategically invested in education to achieve significant success in their career. [Name]'s narrative highlights the symbiotic relationship between education and professional growth.

Subsection 9.2: [Another Name] - Lifelong Learning as a Career Advantage
Learn from the experiences of [Another Name], who embraced lifelong learning as a core career strategy. [Another Name]'s story illustrates the transformative impact of continuous education on personal development and career advancement.

Strategies for Effective Educational Investment:

Section 10: Developing a Personalized Learning Plan

Subsection 10.1: Goal Setting and Educational Planning
Developing a personalized learning plan involves setting clear educational goals aligned with career aspirations. Mapping out a strategic educational journey enhances focus and maximizes the impact of educational investments.

Subsection 10.2: Balancing Formal and Informal Learning
A balanced approach that incorporates both formal and informal learning enhances the richness of educational experiences. This holistic strategy fosters a comprehensive skill set and a well-rounded perspective.

Conclusion:

As we conclude this exploration into the transformative power of education, it becomes evident that investing in education is not merely a financial decision but a commitment to personal and professional growth. Education serves as a gateway to success, unlocking opportunities, fostering innovation, and empowering individuals to navigate the complexities of an ever-evolving world.

In the forthcoming chapters, we will delve deeper into specific aspects of career development, financial planning, and personal empowerment, building upon the foundation laid by the investment in education. The journey towards success is dynamic, and education remains a constant companion on this transformative path.

Chapter 7: Building Skills for the Future - Adapting to Market Trends

In an era marked by rapid technological advancements and evolving industries, the ability to adapt to market trends through skill development is imperative for sustained professional relevance. This chapter delves into the dynamic landscape of building skills for the future, exploring strategies to navigate emerging trends, foster innovation, and remain agile in an ever-changing job market.

The Evolution of Skill Requirements:

Section 1: Understanding Market Dynamics

Subsection 1.1: The Acceleration of Change
Technological advancements, globalization, and industry shifts contribute to the accelerated pace of change in the job market. Understanding the dynamics of these changes is crucial for individuals seeking to proactively adapt their skill sets.

Subsection 1.2: The Impact of Automation and Artificial Intelligence

Automation and artificial intelligence (AI) are reshaping industries and job roles. While they automate routine tasks, they also create opportunities for individuals to focus on higher-order skills such as critical thinking, creativity, and emotional intelligence.

Identifying Future-Proof Skills:

Section 2: Core Skills for the Future

Subsection 2.1: Critical Thinking and Problem-Solving

Critical thinking and problem-solving skills are foundational in navigating complex challenges. Individuals who can analyze information, think critically, and devise innovative solutions are well-positioned for success in evolving industries.

Subsection 2.2: Creativity and Innovation

Creativity and innovation drive progress in dynamic environments. The ability to think creatively, generate novel ideas, and contribute to innovation ensures that individuals remain at the forefront of industry trends.

Subsection 2.3: Emotional Intelligence

In a digitally connected world, emotional intelligence is increasingly recognized as a valuable skill. Individuals with strong emotional intelligence can navigate interpersonal dynamics, build effective relationships, and thrive in collaborative work environments.

Section 3: Technical Proficiency in High-Demand Areas

Subsection 3.1: Data Science and Analytics

The rise of big data necessitates skills in data science and analytics. Proficiency in interpreting data, deriving insights, and making data-driven decisions is a sought-after skill set across various industries.

Subsection 3.2: Digital Literacy and Information Technology

Digital literacy and IT proficiency are fundamental in an era dominated by technology. Individuals adept at leveraging digital tools, understanding cybersecurity, and staying updated on IT trends are equipped for success.

Section 4: Adaptability and Continuous Learning

Subsection 4.1: Cultivating Adaptability
Adaptability is a cornerstone skill for the future. Individuals who embrace change, continuously learn, and adapt to evolving circumstances position themselves as valuable assets in a dynamic job market.

Subsection 4.2: Lifelong Learning Mindset
The commitment to lifelong learning ensures that individuals remain agile in the face of technological advancements. Embracing a mindset of continuous learning enables the acquisition of new skills and the ability to stay ahead of industry trends.

Strategies for Skill Development:

Section 5: Formal Education and Professional Development

Subsection 5.1: Pursuing Relevant Degrees and Certifications
Formal education, including degrees and certifications, remains a structured pathway for skill development. Individuals can strategically pursue education that aligns with emerging industry needs and future-proof their careers.

Subsection 5.2: Professional Development Opportunities
Engaging in professional development opportunities, such as workshops, seminars, and industry conferences, enhances skill sets and provides exposure to the latest trends. Networking within these forums also opens doors to collaboration and mentorship.

Section 6: Online Learning Platforms and MOOCs

Subsection 6.1: Leveraging Online Learning

Online learning platforms and Massive Open Online Courses (MOOCs) offer accessible and flexible avenues for skill development. Individuals can choose from a plethora of courses covering diverse topics, tailoring their learning journey to specific needs.

Subsection 6.2: Microlearning and Bite-Sized Content

Microlearning, characterized by short, focused learning modules, caters to busy professionals. Bite-sized content allows individuals to acquire knowledge incrementally, making it easier to integrate learning into their daily routines.

Industry-Specific Skill Development:

Section 7: Tailoring Skills to Industry Trends

Subsection 7.1: Researching Industry Trends

Understanding industry trends is essential for targeted skill development. Individuals can stay informed by researching market dynamics, attending industry events, and subscribing to relevant publications.

Subsection 7.2: Networking with Industry Professionals

Networking with professionals in the industry provides insights into the specific skills in demand. Engaging with industry communities fosters collaborative learning and opens avenues for mentorship.

Fostering a Culture of Innovation:

Section 8: Entrepreneurial Mindset and Innovation

Subsection 8.1: Cultivating an Entrepreneurial Mindset

An entrepreneurial mindset encourages individuals to approach challenges with creativity and a willingness to take calculated risks. This mindset fosters innovation, making individuals valuable contributors to organizational growth.

Subsection 8.2: Intrapreneurship within Organizations
Intrapreneurship, or entrepreneurship within an organization, empowers individuals to champion innovative projects. Organizations that foster a culture of intrapreneurship tap into the creative potential of their workforce.

Realizing Skills in Action:

Section 9: Case Studies - Exemplifying Skill Development

Subsection 9.1: [Name] - From Skill Development to Industry Leadership
Explore the journey of [Name], an individual who strategically developed in-demand skills and ascended to a leadership role in their industry. [Name]'s story exemplifies the transformative power of skill development.

Subsection 9.2: [Another Name] - Adapting Skills in a Dynamic Environment
Learn from the experiences of [Another Name], who adeptly adapted their skill set to navigate changes in their industry. [Another Name]'s narrative demonstrates the importance of flexibility and continuous learning.

Strategies for Personalized Skill Roadmaps:

Section 10: Crafting Personalized Skill Roadmaps

Subsection 10.1: Self-Assessment and Goal Setting
Crafting personalized skill roadmaps begins with self-assessment. Individuals can identify their strengths, areas for improvement, and align their goals with industry demands.

Subsection 10.2: Iterative Skill Development Plans

Skill development is an iterative process. Individuals can create dynamic plans that evolve based on industry trends, feedback, and personal growth, ensuring continuous alignment with market demands.

Conclusion:

As we conclude this exploration into building skills for the future, it becomes clear that adaptability, innovation, and continuous learning are the cornerstones of professional success. The evolving job market demands individuals to proactively shape their skill sets, positioning themselves as agile contributors to the dynamic landscape of industries.

In the upcoming chapters, we will delve deeper into the practical applications of these skills in various professional contexts, offering actionable insights and strategies for individuals to thrive in the ever-changing world of work. The journey towards building future-proof skills is not only a professional necessity but a transformative pursuit that empowers individuals to excel in their careers and contribute meaningfully to the organizations they serve.

Chapter 8: Financial Planning - The Cornerstone of Long-Term Success

Financial planning is not just a matter of managing money; it is the art of sculpting a secure and prosperous future. In this chapter, we delve into the critical role of financial planning as the cornerstone of long-term success. From budgeting to investments, retirement planning to wealth building, this chapter offers comprehensive insights and strategies to empower individuals on their journey to financial stability and freedom.

Understanding the Fundamentals:

Section 1: The Essence of Financial Planning

Subsection 1.1: Defining Financial Planning

Financial planning is a holistic approach to managing finances, encompassing budgeting, saving, investing, and strategic decision-making to achieve long-term financial goals. It involves aligning financial resources with individual aspirations for a secure future.

Subsection 1.2: The Importance of Financial Literacy

Financial literacy is the foundation of effective financial planning. Understanding concepts such as budgeting, investing, and debt management empowers individuals to make informed decisions that contribute to their financial well-being.

Building a Solid Financial Foundation:

Section 2: Budgeting and Expense Management

Subsection 2.1: Creating a Budget

A budget serves as the roadmap for financial success. Creating a comprehensive budget involves categorizing income, outlining expenses, and identifying areas for savings. Budgeting ensures financial resources are allocated efficiently.

Subsection 2.2: Smart Expense Management

Effective expense management involves evaluating discretionary and non-discretionary spending, identifying cost-saving opportunities, and adopting frugal habits. This disciplined approach frees up resources for saving and investing.

Section 3: Emergency Funds and Financial Resilience

Subsection 3.1: The Importance of Emergency Funds

Emergency funds act as financial safety nets, providing a cushion in times of unexpected expenses or income disruptions. Establishing and maintaining an emergency fund is a key component of financial resilience.

Subsection 3.2: Mitigating Financial Risks

Financial planning includes strategies to mitigate risks, such as securing insurance coverage for health, property, and life. These safeguards protect individuals and families from unforeseen financial burdens.

Investing for Long-Term Growth:

Section 4: Investment Strategies

Subsection 4.1: Setting Investment Goals
Investment goals vary, from short-term objectives to long-term wealth building. Defining clear investment goals guides individuals in selecting appropriate investment vehicles aligned with their risk tolerance and time horizon.

Subsection 4.2: Diversification and Risk Management
Diversification, spreading investments across different asset classes, is a fundamental risk management strategy. It minimizes the impact of poor-performing assets and enhances the potential for long-term returns.

Section 5: Retirement Planning

Subsection 5.1: The Importance of Early Planning
Retirement planning is a marathon, not a sprint. Early planning allows individuals to harness the power of compounding, contributing smaller amounts over a longer period to build substantial retirement savings.

Subsection 5.2: Understanding Retirement Accounts
Navigating retirement accounts, such as 401(k)s and IRAs, is crucial. Maximizing contributions, taking advantage of employer matches, and optimizing tax benefits are essential components of effective retirement planning.

Strategies for Debt Management:

Section 6: Responsible Debt Management

Subsection 6.1: Differentiating Between Good and Bad Debt

Not all debts are created equal. Understanding the distinction between good debt (investments with potential returns) and bad debt (high-interest consumer debt) informs strategic debt management decisions.

Subsection 6.2: Creating a Debt Repayment Plan

Developing a structured plan to repay debts involves prioritizing high-interest debts, negotiating interest rates, and adopting accelerated repayment strategies. A systematic approach accelerates the journey to debt-free living.

Wealth Building and Financial Independence:

Section 7: Strategies for Wealth Building

Subsection 7.1: Harnessing Passive Income Streams

Passive income streams, such as dividends, real estate investments, and royalties, contribute to long-term wealth building. Diversifying income sources enhances financial stability and accelerates the path to financial independence.

Subsection 7.2: Continual Learning and Financial Adaptability

Financial success is an evolving process. Continual learning about investment opportunities, tax strategies, and market trends ensures individuals adapt their financial plans to capitalize on emerging opportunities.

Advanced Financial Planning Strategies:

Section 8: Estate Planning and Generational Wealth

Subsection 8.1: The Role of Estate Planning

Estate planning involves creating a comprehensive plan for the distribution of assets, minimizing taxes, and ensuring the smooth transfer of wealth to future generations. It safeguards family legacies and minimizes potential disputes.

Subsection 8.2: Generational Wealth Mindset

Generational wealth is built on a mindset of sustainability and legacy. Strategies include education funding, charitable giving, and instilling financial literacy in successive generations to perpetuate wealth responsibly.

Case Studies: Financial Success Stories

Section 9: Real-Life Narratives

Subsection 9.1: [Name] - From Financial Struggle to Independence

Explore the journey of [Name], who transformed financial challenges into opportunities for wealth building. [Name]'s narrative exemplifies the transformative power of strategic financial planning.

Subsection 9.2: [Another Name] - Navigating Market Volatility

Learn from the experiences of [Another Name], who navigated market volatility with resilience and strategic financial planning. [Another Name]'s story underscores the importance of adaptability in financial success.

Navigating Economic Changes:

Section 10: Financial Resilience in Economic Downturns

Subsection 10.1: Building a Robust Financial Safety Net

Economic downturns are inevitable. Building a robust financial safety net, including emergency funds and conservative investments, fortifies individuals against the impact of economic uncertainties.

Subsection 10.2: Strategic Decision-Making in Tough Times

Strategic decision-making during economic challenges involves reassessing financial goals, cutting non-essential expenses, and seizing investment opportunities. Prudent actions during downturns position individuals for long-term success.

The Future of Financial Planning:

Section 11: Embracing Technological Tools

Subsection 11.1: Leveraging Financial Technology

Financial technology (FinTech) tools offer innovative solutions for budgeting, investing, and financial management. Embracing these technologies enhances the efficiency and accessibility of financial planning.

Subsection 11.2: Evolving with Digital Currencies

The rise of digital currencies prompts individuals to explore their role in financial planning. Understanding the potential benefits and risks of digital currencies is crucial for adapting to the evolving financial landscape.

Conclusion:

As we conclude this exploration into financial planning, it is evident that strategic financial management is not just a task; it is a lifelong commitment to building a foundation of stability and prosperity. From the basics of budgeting to advanced wealth-building strategies, each aspect contributes to the holistic goal of

Chapter 9: Real Estate - Your Ultimate Asset

Real estate stands as a tangible testament to the enduring value of property ownership. In this chapter, we embark on a comprehensive exploration of real estate as the ultimate asset. From the advantages of homeownership to the potential of real estate investments, this chapter unravels the intricacies of leveraging real estate for long-term financial growth, stability, and wealth accumulation.

Embracing Homeownership:

Section 1: The Advantages of Homeownership

Subsection 1.1: Building Equity Through Homeownership
Homeownership is a cornerstone of wealth accumulation. As mortgage payments contribute to property equity, homeownership serves as a long-term investment that can appreciate over time, providing financial stability and security.

Subsection 1.2: Stability and Emotional Fulfillment
Owning a home fosters stability, both financially and emotionally. The sense of belonging and control over one's living space contributes to a fulfilling and anchored lifestyle, impacting overall well-being.

Navigating Residential Real Estate:

Section 2: Home Buying Strategies

Subsection 2.1: Financial Preparedness for Home Purchase

Strategic financial planning is essential before venturing into homeownership. Understanding credit scores, securing pre-approval, and assessing budget constraints contribute to a successful home-buying journey.

Subsection 2.2: Selecting the Right Property

Choosing the right property involves considering location, amenities, and potential for appreciation. A thoughtful selection aligns the property with personal and financial goals, maximizing the value of the real estate investment.

Section 3: Financing Your Home

Subsection 3.1: Mortgage Options and Considerations

Navigating mortgage options requires an understanding of fixed-rate and adjustable-rate mortgages, as well as government-backed loan programs. Tailoring mortgage choices to individual financial situations optimizes the benefits of homeownership.

Subsection 3.2: Managing Down Payments and Closing Costs

Effectively managing down payments and closing costs is integral to the home-buying process. Strategies for saving, negotiating, and exploring assistance programs contribute to a financially viable real estate transaction.

Unleashing the Potential of Real Estate Investments:

Section 4: Real Estate Investments Overview

Subsection 4.1: The Wealth-Building Power of Real Estate Investments

Real estate investments offer a robust avenue for wealth building. Whether through rental properties, real estate investment trusts (REITs), or property development, strategic investments provide avenues for generating income and appreciation.

Subsection 4.2: Diversification through Real Estate

Diversifying investment portfolios with real estate mitigates risk and enhances long-term financial stability. Real estate investments, with their potential for consistent returns and tax advantages, serve as a valuable complement to traditional investment vehicles.

Section 5: Rental Properties - Passive Income and Wealth Creation

Subsection 5.1: Becoming a Successful Landlord

Owning rental properties opens doors to passive income streams. Successful property management involves selecting the right tenants, maintaining properties, and navigating the legal aspects of landlord-tenant relationships.

Subsection 5.2: Tax Benefits of Rental Property Ownership

Understanding the tax benefits associated with rental property ownership is crucial. Deductions for mortgage interest, property depreciation, and operating expenses enhance the financial appeal of real estate investments.

Commercial Real Estate Ventures:

Section 6: Exploring Commercial Real Estate

Subsection 6.1: The Dynamics of Commercial Real Estate

Commercial real estate ventures offer unique opportunities for wealth creation. From office spaces to retail properties, understanding the dynamics of commercial real estate allows investors to capitalize on diverse market segments.

Subsection 6.2: Risks and Rewards of Commercial Investments

While commercial real estate presents lucrative prospects, it also involves inherent risks. Evaluating market trends, tenant stability, and economic indicators is essential for making informed decisions and mitigating potential challenges.

Strategies for Real Estate Success:

Section 7: Developing a Real Estate Investment Plan

Subsection 7.1: Setting Investment Objectives
Defining clear investment objectives guides the development of a real estate investment plan. Whether focused on rental income, property appreciation, or portfolio diversification, aligning strategies with goals is paramount.

Subsection 7.2: Risk Management in Real Estate
Real estate investments, like any other asset class, carry risks. Implementing risk management strategies, such as thorough due diligence, diversification, and staying informed about market trends, safeguards investments.

Section 8: Financing Real Estate Investments

Subsection 8.1: Creative Financing Techniques
Creative financing techniques, including leveraging other assets, exploring partnerships, and understanding alternative lending options, offer flexibility in financing real estate investments.

Subsection 8.2: Calculating Returns and Assessing Investment Performance
Calculating returns on real estate investments involves evaluating metrics such as return on investment (ROI), cash flow, and appreciation. Regularly assessing investment performance allows investors to make informed adjustments to their strategies.

Real Estate Market Trends and Forecasts:

Section 9: Adapting to Market Trends

Subsection 9.1: Embracing Technological Advancements in Real Estate
Technological advancements, from virtual property tours to blockchain in real estate transactions, shape market trends. Embracing technology enhances efficiency, transparency, and accessibility in real estate transactions.

Subsection 9.2: Navigating Market Cycles
Real estate markets undergo cycles influenced by economic factors. Navigating market cycles involves strategic buying or selling decisions, adapting to changing demand, and identifying emerging opportunities.

Real Estate Case Studies:

Section 10: Real-Life Success Stories

Subsection 10.1: [Name] - From First-Time Homebuyer to Real Estate Mogul
Explore the journey of [Name], who transitioned from being a first-time homebuyer to a successful real estate investor. [Name]'s story exemplifies the transformative potential of real estate as a wealth-building asset.

Subsection 10.2: [Another Name] - Entrepreneurial Ventures in Commercial Real Estate
Learn from the experiences of [Another Name], who ventured into commercial real estate with entrepreneurial acumen. [Another Name]'s narrative sheds light on the strategies and challenges involved in commercial real estate endeavors.

Ethical Considerations and Sustainable Real Estate:

Section 11: Ethical Real Estate Practices

Subsection 11.1: Responsible Property Management

Responsible property management involves ethical considerations such as fair housing practices, transparent communication with tenants, and adhering to legal standards. Upholding ethical practices fosters a positive reputation and sustainable success.

Subsection 11.2: Sustainable Real Estate Development
Sustainable real estate development prioritizes environmentally conscious practices, energy efficiency, and community impact. Investors and developers committed to sustainability contribute to long-term ecological and social well-being

Chapter 10: Side Hustles and Passive Income - Multiplying Your Earnings

In a world driven by innovation and entrepreneurial spirit, the concept of earning income has expanded beyond traditional avenues. This chapter delves into the transformative power of side hustles and passive income, exploring how individuals can leverage additional streams of revenue to multiply their earnings, achieve financial goals, and create a pathway to financial freedom.

Understanding the Landscape:

Section 1: The Rise of Side Hustles

Subsection 1.1: Defining Side Hustles
Side hustles are supplemental income streams pursued alongside a primary job or commitment. The rise of side hustles reflects a shift in the workforce towards diversified income strategies and entrepreneurial endeavors.

Subsection 1.2: The Gig Economy and Freelancing

The gig economy and freelancing platforms have democratized opportunities for individuals to monetize their skills and talents. Access to a global marketplace allows for the creation of diverse and lucrative side hustles.

Exploring Side Hustle Opportunities:

Section 2: Identifying Your Skills and Passions

Subsection 2.1: Leveraging Skills for Side Hustles

Identifying and leveraging existing skills is a foundational step in side hustle exploration. Whether it's graphic design, writing, coding, or other talents, aligning side hustles with personal proficiencies enhances success.

Subsection 2.2: Pursuing Passion Projects

Side hustles driven by passion not only provide fulfillment but also increase the likelihood of sustained commitment and success. Aligning income-generating activities with personal interests fosters creativity and dedication.

Section 3: Side Hustle Ideas for Different Professions

Subsection 3.1: Side Hustles for Creatives

Creatives can explore side hustles such as freelance writing, graphic design, photography, or selling digital art. Online platforms provide avenues for showcasing and monetizing creative talents.

Subsection 3.2: Tech-Based Side Hustles

Individuals with tech skills can venture into side hustles like app development, website design, or digital marketing. The tech industry offers a plethora of opportunities for generating supplemental income.

Section 4: Building an Online Presence

Subsection 4.1: Personal Branding for Side Hustles

Establishing a strong personal brand enhances the visibility and credibility of side hustles.

Leveraging social media, personal websites, and professional profiles creates an online presence

that attracts clients and customers.

Subsection 4.2: Utilizing E-Commerce Platforms

E-commerce platforms offer accessible avenues for selling products, services, or digital goods.

Setting up an online store allows individuals to reach a global audience and monetize their offerings.

The Power of Passive Income:

Section 5: Passive Income Strategies

Subsection 5.1: Investing for Passive Income

Investing in dividend-paying stocks, real estate, or peer-to-peer lending can generate passive income.

Strategic investment decisions contribute to a steady stream of earnings with minimal ongoing

effort.

Subsection 5.2: Creating and Selling Digital Products

Digital products, such as e-books, online courses, or stock photography, offer opportunities for

passive income. Once created, these products can be sold repeatedly without significant ongoing

involvement.

Section 6: Real Estate Investments for Passive Income

Subsection 6.1: Rental Properties as Passive Income Streams

Owning and renting out properties provides a consistent source of passive income. Effective

property management and understanding the rental market contribute to successful real

estate-based passive income.

Subsection 6.2: Real Estate Crowdfunding

Real estate crowdfunding platforms enable individuals to invest in property projects collectively. This approach allows for passive income generation without the direct responsibilities of property ownership.

Strategies for Success:

Section 7: Time Management and Goal Setting

Subsection 7.1: Balancing Side Hustles with Main Commitments
Effectively managing time is crucial when juggling side hustles with primary commitments. Setting realistic goals and priorities ensures a balanced approach that aligns with overall financial objectives.

Subsection 7.2: Creating Long-Term Strategies
Long-term success in side hustles requires strategic planning. Developing a roadmap that includes scaling, diversification, and adapting to market trends ensures sustained growth and profitability.

Section 8: Financial Planning for Side Hustles

Subsection 8.1: Budgeting and Tax Considerations
Incorporating side hustle income into personal financial planning involves effective budgeting and tax considerations. Understanding tax obligations and optimizing budget allocation maximize the benefits of additional income.

Subsection 8.2: Emergency Funds for Side Hustle Ventures
Maintaining emergency funds specific to side hustle ventures safeguards against financial uncertainties. Having a financial buffer allows individuals to navigate challenges and seize opportunities for side hustle growth.

Real-Life Side Hustle Stories:

Section 9: Inspirational Narratives

Subsection 9.1: [Name] - Turning a Side Passion into Profit

Explore the journey of [Name], who transformed a hobby into a lucrative side hustle. [Name]'s story illustrates how pursuing one's passions can lead to both personal fulfillment and financial success.

Subsection 9.2: [Another Name] - Scaling a Side Hustle into a Business

Learn from the experiences of [Another Name], who turned a small side hustle into a full-fledged business. [Another Name]'s narrative highlights the potential for growth and expansion in entrepreneurial endeavors.

Challenges and Solutions:

Section 10: Overcoming Side Hustle Challenges

Subsection 10.1: Managing Burnout and Fatigue

Juggling multiple responsibilities can lead to burnout. Implementing self-care practices, setting realistic expectations, and periodically reassessing commitments help manage burnout and fatigue.

Subsection 10.2: Adapting to Market Changes

The business landscape is dynamic, requiring individuals to adapt to market changes. Staying informed, fostering agility, and diversifying side hustle ventures mitigate the impact of external shifts.

Future Trends in Side Hustles and Passive Income:

Section 11: Emerging Opportunities

Subsection 11.1: The Role of Technology

Technological advancements continue to shape the landscape of side hustles. Embracing emerging technologies, such as artificial intelligence and blockchain, opens new frontiers for income-generating activities.

Subsection 11.2: Sustainable and Socially Responsible Side Hustles
The

Chapter 11: Balancing Act - Work-Life Harmony for Sustainable Success

Achieving sustainable success is not just about professional accomplishments but also about maintaining a harmonious balance between work and life. In this chapter, we explore the art of finding equilibrium, managing stress, and fostering personal well-being to ensure long-term success in both professional and personal realms.

The Importance of Work-Life Harmony:

Section 1: Defining Work-Life Harmony

Subsection 1.1: Beyond Work-Life Balance
Work-life harmony goes beyond the traditional concept of work-life balance. It emphasizes an integrated approach where work and personal life complement each other, creating a seamless and fulfilling existence.

Subsection 1.2: The Impact on Overall Well-Being

Achieving work-life harmony positively impacts mental, emotional, and physical well-being. It promotes a sense of fulfillment, reduces stress, and enhances overall life satisfaction.

Navigating Professional Responsibilities:

Section 2: Efficient Time Management

Subsection 2.1: Prioritizing Tasks and Responsibilities

Effective time management involves prioritizing tasks based on importance and deadlines. Identifying key responsibilities and allocating time strategically contributes to both professional success and personal well-being.

Subsection 2.2: Setting Realistic Goals

Setting realistic and achievable goals prevents overwhelm. Balancing ambition with feasibility ensures that professional objectives align with the capacity for sustained effort and performance.

Section 3: Establishing Boundaries

Subsection 3.1: Defining Work and Personal Boundaries

Establishing clear boundaries between work and personal life is crucial. This includes setting limits on work hours, designating specific spaces for work, and creating routines that facilitate a smooth transition between professional and personal spheres.

Subsection 3.2: Saying No When Necessary

Learning to say no is a powerful skill in maintaining work-life harmony. Prioritizing tasks and commitments helps in discerning when to decline additional responsibilities, preserving time and energy for essential aspects of life.

Fostering a Positive Work Environment:

Section 4: Cultivating a Supportive Workplace Culture

Subsection 4.1: Encouraging Flexibility and Autonomy
Workplaces that embrace flexibility and autonomy contribute to work-life harmony. Allowing employees to choose when and where they work fosters a sense of control over their professional lives.

Subsection 4.2: Promoting Open Communication
Open communication channels between employers and employees create an environment where concerns, expectations, and work-related challenges can be discussed openly. This transparency promotes mutual understanding and collaboration.

Section 5: Leveraging Technology for Efficiency

Subsection 5.1: Using Technology Wisely
Technology can be a double-edged sword. While it enhances productivity, it can also contribute to a constant sense of connectivity. Setting boundaries on technology use and adopting tools that streamline tasks contribute to a more efficient work environment.

Subsection 5.2: Embracing Remote Work Opportunities
Remote work provides flexibility but requires intentional efforts to maintain work-life boundaries. Implementing strategies for effective remote work, such as designated workspaces and defined work hours, ensures a balanced approach.

Prioritizing Personal Well-Being:

Section 6: Mental and Emotional Health

Subsection 6.1: Stress Management Techniques
Stress is an inevitable part of professional life. Employing stress management techniques, such as mindfulness, meditation, and regular breaks, helps individuals cope with work-related pressures.

Subsection 6.2: Seeking Professional Support

Acknowledging the importance of mental health includes seeking professional support when needed. Employee assistance programs, counseling services, and mental health resources contribute to a supportive work environment.

Section 7: Physical Well-Being Practices

Subsection 7.1: Incorporating Physical Activity

Regular physical activity is essential for overall well-being. Encouraging employees to incorporate exercise into their routines contributes to improved physical health, increased energy levels, and stress reduction.

Subsection 7.2: Prioritizing Sleep

Adequate sleep is fundamental to cognitive function and emotional resilience. Employers can support work-life harmony by fostering a culture that values and prioritizes sufficient sleep.

Balancing Family and Professional Commitments:

Section 8: Parental and Caregiving Responsibilities

Subsection 8.1: Supporting Parental Leave Policies

Employers can contribute to work-life harmony by implementing supportive parental leave policies. Providing adequate time for parents to bond with their children promotes a healthy balance between work and family life.

Subsection 8.2: Flexibility for Caregivers

Recognizing the responsibilities of caregivers, whether for children or elderly family members, involves offering flexibility in work schedules and understanding the unique challenges they face.

Section 9: Creating Family-Centric Workplaces

Subsection 9.1: On-Site Childcare Facilities

Workplaces can enhance work-life harmony by providing on-site childcare facilities. This proactive approach supports working parents by offering convenience and peace of mind.

Subsection 9.2: Family-Friendly Events and Policies
Organizing family-friendly events and implementing policies that accommodate family commitments create an inclusive and supportive workplace culture.

Strategies for Entrepreneurs and Small Business Owners:

Section 10: Navigating Entrepreneurial Challenges

Subsection 10.1: Delegating Responsibilities
Entrepreneurs and small business owners often wear multiple hats. Delegating responsibilities and building a reliable team are critical for preventing burnout and achieving work-life harmony.

Subsection 10.2: Creating Boundaries as a Business Owner
Establishing boundaries as a business owner involves setting realistic expectations for oneself and the team. Clear communication about availability and defining non-negotiable personal time contribute to a balanced entrepreneurial life.

Work-Life Harmony Case Studies:

Section 11: Success Stories

Subsection 11.1: [Name] - Finding Balance in a Demanding Career
Explore the journey of [Name], who navigated a demanding career while maintaining a harmonious work-life balance. [Name]'s story serves as inspiration for those seeking equilibrium in their professional and personal lives.

Subsection 11.2: [Another Name] - Entrepreneurial Triumph with Work-Life Harmony

Learn from the experiences of [Another Name], an entrepreneur who built a successful business while prioritizing work-life harmony. [Another Name]'s narrative provides insights into the strategies that contributed to both professional and personal fulfillment.

Future Trends in Work-Life Harmony:

Section 12: Adapting to Evolving Work Environments

Subsection 12.1: Remote Work as a Permanent Fixture
The shift towards remote work may continue, requiring individuals and employers to adapt to a new normal. Strategies for maintaining work-life harmony in a remote work environment will be crucial.

Subsection 12.2: Embracing Flexibility and Employee Well-Being
Future work environments are likely to prioritize flexibility and employee well-being. Companies that proactively address work-life harmony as a strategic priority will attract and retain top talent.

Chapter 12: Legacy Building - Ensuring Prosperity for the Next Generation

Legacy building is a timeless pursuit that transcends personal success, aiming to secure prosperity for generations to come. This chapter delves into the multifaceted aspects of creating a lasting legacy, encompassing financial planning, education, values, and the preservation of wealth for the enrichment of future generations.

Understanding the Significance of Legacy:

Section 1: Defining Legacy in a Broader Context

Subsection 1.1: Beyond Material Wealth
Legacy extends beyond material wealth; it encompasses values, traditions, and the impact one leaves on the community and the world. Understanding the broader context of legacy building sets the foundation for a purposeful journey.

Subsection 1.2: The Intergenerational Impact

A well-crafted legacy has the power to positively influence not only the immediate descendants but also subsequent generations. Intergenerational impact involves imparting wisdom, instilling values, and fostering a sense of responsibility towards society.

Financial Planning for Long-Term Prosperity:

Section 2: Strategic Wealth Management

Subsection 2.1: Multi-Generational Financial Planning
Legacy building necessitates strategic financial planning that spans multiple generations. This involves wealth preservation, tax optimization, and the creation of trusts and structures designed to sustain and grow family assets.

Subsection 2.2: Investment Strategies for Long-Term Growth
Investing with a focus on long-term growth is a fundamental component of legacy building. Diversifying investments, considering risk tolerance, and adapting to market trends ensure the resilience and growth of family wealth.

Section 3: Estate Planning and Succession

Subsection 3.1: Crafting Comprehensive Estate Plans
Estate planning involves more than distributing assets; it includes minimizing taxes, managing liabilities, and ensuring a smooth transfer of wealth. A comprehensive estate plan is crucial for preserving the family legacy.

Subsection 3.2: Succession Planning for Businesses
For family businesses, effective succession planning is paramount. Identifying and preparing the next generation of leaders, while maintaining the core values of the business, ensures its continued success and contribution to the family legacy.

Education as a Cornerstone:

Section 4: Investing in Educational Opportunities

Subsection 4.1: Funding Higher Education

Supporting higher education for descendants opens doors to opportunities and empowers them to contribute meaningfully to society. Establishing education funds and scholarship programs are impactful ways to invest in the intellectual capital of the family.

Subsection 4.2: Fostering a Culture of Lifelong Learning

Beyond formal education, fostering a culture of lifelong learning within the family instills curiosity, adaptability, and a commitment to continuous improvement. This mindset becomes a legacy in itself, perpetuating a thirst for knowledge through generations.

Instilling Values and Ethics:

Section 5: Passing Down Core Values

Subsection 5.1: Articulating Family Values

Defining and articulating core family values provides a moral compass for descendants. These values become the guiding principles that shape decisions, relationships, and the overall conduct of family members.

Subsection 5.2: Ethical Leadership and Social Responsibility

Legacy building involves instilling a sense of ethical leadership and social responsibility. Encouraging family members to contribute to community development, philanthropy, and ethical business practices ensures a positive impact on the world.

Philanthropy and Social Impact:

Section 6: Establishing Family Foundations

Subsection 6.1: Creating a Philanthropic Legacy

Establishing family foundations allows for organized and impactful philanthropy. It enables the family to support causes aligned with their values, leaving a lasting legacy of positive social impact.

Subsection 6.2: Engaging the Family in Philanthropy
Involving family members in philanthropic activities fosters a sense of unity and shared purpose. Collaborative decision-making on charitable initiatives strengthens family bonds while contributing to the greater good.

Preserving Cultural Heritage:

Section 7: Cultural Preservation and Heritage

Subsection 7.1: Documenting Family History
Preserving family history through documentation ensures that traditions, stories, and cultural heritage are passed down through generations. This creates a sense of identity and belonging for descendants.

Subsection 7.2: Supporting Cultural Initiatives
Investing in cultural initiatives, whether through art, literature, or community projects, contributes to the preservation and enrichment of cultural heritage. This legacy transcends financial wealth, leaving an enduring mark on society.

Strategies for Family Unity:

Section 8: Nurturing Family Bonds

Subsection 8.1: Family Retreats and Traditions
Organizing family retreats and establishing traditions create opportunities for bonding and the transmission of values. These shared experiences strengthen the familial connection and contribute to a cohesive legacy.

Subsection 8.2: Effective Communication Practices

Open and effective communication is the glue that binds generations. Implementing communication practices, such as regular family meetings and the use of technology to stay connected, fosters understanding and unity.

Managing Challenges and Conflicts:

Section 9: Conflict Resolution Strategies

Subsection 9.1: Navigating Inter-Generational Conflicts

Conflict is inevitable in family dynamics. Implementing effective conflict resolution strategies, such as mediation and open dialogue, prevents disputes from jeopardizing the unity required for successful legacy building.

Subsection 9.2: Professional Guidance for Family Governance

Engaging professional advisors, such as family business consultants and estate planners, can provide objective insights and frameworks for effective family governance. This external guidance ensures that challenges are addressed proactively.

Case Studies in Successful Legacy Building:

Section 10: Exemplary Family Legacies

Subsection 10.1: [Name] Family - Sustaining a Legacy of Innovation

Explore the story of the [Name] family, which has sustained a legacy of innovation through generations. This case study examines how their commitment to creativity and entrepreneurial spirit has shaped their enduring impact.

Subsection 10.2: [Another Name] Family - Balancing Tradition and Modernity

Discover how the [Another Name] family has successfully balanced tradition and modernity in building their legacy. This case study explores their strategies for preserving cultural heritage while adapting to the evolving world.

Future-Proofing the Family Legacy:

Section 11: Adapting to Evolving Dynamics

Subsection 11.1: Embracing Technological Advancements
Incorporating technology into legacy-building strategies ensures relevance in a rapidly changing world. Embracing digital tools for education, communication, and financial management positions the family to adapt to future challenges.

Subsection 11.2: Environmental and Sustainable Practices
Future-proofing the family legacy involves considering environmental sustainability. Integrating eco-friendly practices and investments in sustainable initiatives contribute to a legacy that prioritizes the well-being of the planet.

Chapter 13: Mastering the Art of Networking - Opening Doors to Opportunities

Networking is an art that transcends traditional professional connections, encompassing a vast landscape of opportunities. This chapter explores the nuances of networking, offering insights into building meaningful relationships, leveraging digital platforms, and mastering the art of networking to open doors to diverse and valuable opportunities.

The Essence of Networking:

Section 1: Redefining Networking in the Modern Era

Subsection 1.1: Beyond Business Cards and Handshakes
Networking in the modern era extends beyond traditional practices. It involves building authentic connections, nurturing relationships, and creating a diverse network that goes beyond immediate professional circles.

Subsection 1.2: The Power of Networking in Personal and Professional Growth

Effective networking is a catalyst for personal and professional growth. It opens doors to opportunities, fosters collaboration, and provides a supportive community that contributes to success in various aspects of life.

Building Meaningful Connections:

Section 2: The Art of Relationship Building

Subsection 2.1: Authenticity in Networking

Authenticity is the cornerstone of meaningful connections. Building genuine relationships, rooted in trust and mutual respect, forms the basis for long-lasting professional and personal collaborations.

Subsection 2.2: Listening and Empathy in Networking

Listening actively and approaching networking with empathy enhances the quality of connections. Understanding the needs and aspirations of others creates a foundation for reciprocity and support within the network.

Section 3: Networking Across Industries and Professions

Subsection 3.1: The Power of Cross-Industry Networking

Diversifying networking efforts across various industries brings fresh perspectives and opportunities. Interacting with professionals from different fields fosters innovation and opens doors to unexpected collaborations.

Subsection 3.2: Networking in the Digital Age

Digital platforms provide unprecedented opportunities for cross-industry networking. Leveraging social media, online forums, and virtual events expands the reach of networking initiatives beyond geographical constraints.

Leveraging Digital Platforms:

Section 4: Navigating Social Media for Networking

Subsection 4.1: LinkedIn as a Networking Powerhouse
LinkedIn stands as a central platform for professional networking. Optimizing profiles, engaging in meaningful discussions, and utilizing advanced features unlock the full potential of LinkedIn as a networking tool.

Subsection 4.2: Twitter, Instagram, and Beyond
Beyond LinkedIn, other social media platforms play unique roles in networking. Twitter's real-time conversations and Instagram's visual storytelling offer additional avenues to connect with diverse audiences and build a personal brand.

Section 5: Virtual Networking Best Practices

Subsection 5.1: Making an Impact in Virtual Spaces
Virtual networking has become increasingly prevalent. Strategies for making a memorable impact in virtual spaces, including effective communication and virtual event participation, are crucial in the digital age.

Subsection 5.2: Overcoming Challenges in Virtual Networking
Challenges such as online fatigue and lack of face-to-face interaction are inherent to virtual networking. Implementing strategies to overcome these challenges ensures sustained engagement and effectiveness in the digital networking landscape.

Networking Strategies for Career Advancement:

Section 6: Building a Professional Brand

Subsection 6.1: Crafting an Impactful Personal Brand

A strong personal brand distinguishes professionals in a competitive landscape. Aligning personal values, skills, and aspirations creates a compelling narrative that attracts meaningful connections and opportunities.

Subsection 6.2: Elevator Pitches and Personal Storytelling
Mastering the art of concise and compelling storytelling is essential in networking. Crafting effective elevator pitches and personal stories enables professionals to articulate their value and capture attention in diverse settings.

Section 7: Mentorship and Networking

Subsection 7.1: The Role of Mentors in Networking
Mentorship plays a pivotal role in networking and career development. Establishing mentor-mentee relationships provides guidance, insights, and access to valuable networks that contribute to professional growth.

Subsection 7.2: Paying It Forward through Mentorship
As professionals advance in their careers, engaging in mentorship creates a culture of giving back. Mentoring others not only contributes to the growth of the mentee but also expands the mentor's network and influence.

Networking in Entrepreneurship:

Section 8: Networking for Entrepreneurs

Subsection 8.1: Building a Startup Ecosystem
Entrepreneurs thrive in vibrant startup ecosystems. Actively participating in industry events, connecting with investors, and collaborating with fellow entrepreneurs contribute to creating a robust support system.

Subsection 8.2: Pitching and Fundraising through Networking

Effectively pitching ideas and fundraising often hinge on networking. Developing strong relationships with potential investors, mentors, and collaborators is instrumental in securing support for entrepreneurial ventures.

Navigating Networking Events:

Section 9: Strategies for In-Person Networking

Subsection 9.1: Maximizing Networking Events
In-person networking events remain invaluable for establishing direct connections. Strategies for maximizing these events, including effective communication and strategic planning, enhance the networking experience.

Subsection 9.2: Overcoming Networking Anxiety
Networking anxiety is a common challenge. Practical tips and techniques for overcoming anxiety, such as setting realistic goals and adopting a positive mindset, empower professionals to navigate networking events with confidence.

International Networking and Global Opportunities:

Section 10: Networking on a Global Scale

Subsection 10.1: The Dynamics of International Networking
Navigating international networking involves understanding cultural nuances and adapting communication strategies. Building a global network broadens horizons and opens doors to diverse opportunities.

Subsection 10.2: Digital Nomadism and Global Connectivity
The rise of digital nomadism underscores the importance of global connectivity. Leveraging technology to connect with professionals worldwide and embracing a flexible approach to work enhances international networking efforts.

Measuring Success in Networking:

Section 11: Key Performance Indicators (KPIs) for Networking

Subsection 11.1: Quantifying Networking Success

Measuring the success of networking efforts requires defining key performance indicators (KPIs). Tracking metrics such as the growth of connections, collaboration opportunities, and achieved goals provides tangible insights into networking effectiveness.

Subsection 11.2: Building a Network of Advocates

A network of advocates consists of individuals who actively support and promote one another. Fostering relationships with advocates within the network amplifies opportunities and contributes to sustained professional success.

Case Studies in Networking Excellence:

Section 12: Success Stories in Networking

Subsection 12.1: [Name] - From Networking Novice to Industry Leader

Explore the journey of [Name], who transformed from a networking novice to an industry leader through strategic relationship-building. This case study unveils the specific networking strategies that propelled [Name] to success.

Subsection 12.2: [Another Name] - Leveraging Networking for Global Ventures

Learn from the experiences of [Another Name], an entrepreneur who leveraged networking for global business ventures. This case study highlights the role of international connections and digital platforms in achieving entrepreneurial success.

Ethical Considerations in Networking:

Section 13: Ethics and Integrity in Networking

Subsection 13.1: Navigating Ethical Dilemmas

Ethical dilemmas may arise in networking. Maintaining integrity, transparency, and fairness in interactions with others are essential principles that guide professionals through challenging situations.

Chapter 14: Overcoming Challenges - Resilience in the Face of Adversity

Resilience, the ability to bounce back from setbacks, is a fundamental trait that defines individuals and shapes their journey in the face of adversity. This chapter explores the multifaceted nature of resilience, offering insights into building mental fortitude, navigating personal and professional challenges, and emerging stronger from adversity.

Understanding Resilience:

Section 1: Defining Resilience in a Dynamic World

Subsection 1.1: The Adaptive Nature of Resilience
Resilience is more than just bouncing back; it's an adaptive process that involves learning, growth, and the ability to navigate life's uncertainties. Understanding resilience as a dynamic and evolving trait sets the stage for effective coping mechanisms.

Subsection 1.2: Resilience Across Personal and Professional Arenas

Resilience is a universal quality that transcends personal and professional boundaries. Whether facing setbacks in careers, relationships, or health, the principles of resilience remain applicable, contributing to holistic well-being.

Building Mental Fortitude:

Section 2: Cultivating a Resilient Mindset

Subsection 2.1: The Power of Positive Thinking

Positive thinking is a foundational element of resilience. Cultivating an optimistic mindset enables individuals to reframe challenges as opportunities for growth, fostering mental fortitude in the face of adversity.

Subsection 2.2: Embracing Change and Uncertainty

Resilient individuals embrace change and uncertainty as inherent aspects of life. Adapting to new circumstances and viewing challenges as part of the journey contribute to a mindset that thrives in dynamic environments.

Section 3: Developing Emotional Intelligence

Subsection 3.1: Understanding and Regulating Emotions

Emotional intelligence plays a crucial role in resilience. Recognizing and regulating emotions empower individuals to respond to challenges in a balanced and constructive manner, promoting mental well-being.

Subsection 3.2: Fostering Interpersonal Relationships

Strong interpersonal relationships provide a support system during challenging times. Building and nurturing connections with others enhance emotional resilience, creating a network that contributes to overall mental health.

Navigating Personal Challenges:

Section 4: Resilience in Health and Well-Being

Subsection 4.1: Coping with Physical Health Challenges
Maintaining resilience in the face of physical health challenges involves a holistic approach. Integrating healthy lifestyle choices, seeking medical support, and cultivating a positive mindset contribute to overall well-being.

Subsection 4.2: Mental Health and Resilience
Resilience is closely tied to mental health. Addressing mental health challenges involves destigmatizing seeking support, building coping mechanisms, and creating environments that prioritize emotional well-being.

Section 5: Relationships and Family Resilience

Subsection 5.1: Navigating Relationship Struggles
Resilient individuals navigate relationship challenges with empathy and effective communication. Building resilience in relationships involves mutual support, conflict resolution skills, and a commitment to growth together.

Subsection 5.2: Family as a Source of Strength
Families can serve as a powerful source of resilience. Fostering open communication, maintaining shared values, and supporting one another create a foundation for family resilience in times of adversity.

Resilience in the Professional Sphere:

Section 6: Overcoming Career Setbacks

Subsection 6.1: Job Loss and Career Transitions

Resilience is essential when facing job loss or navigating career transitions. Developing a proactive approach, acquiring new skills, and leveraging networks contribute to resilience in the professional sphere.

Subsection 6.2: Thriving in a Competitive Workplace
The competitive nature of workplaces requires resilience. Developing a growth mindset, seeking feedback, and adapting to industry changes position individuals to thrive and overcome challenges in their careers.

Section 7: Entrepreneurial Resilience

Subsection 7.1: Weathering Business Challenges
Entrepreneurs encounter numerous challenges in the dynamic business landscape. Building entrepreneurial resilience involves strategic planning, risk management, and the ability to learn and pivot in response to setbacks.

Subsection 7.2: Bouncing Back from Business Failures
Resilience is particularly critical when facing business failures. Entrepreneurs who view failures as learning experiences, pivot strategically, and maintain a resilient mindset are more likely to achieve long-term success.

Strategies for Cultivating Resilience:

Section 8: Mindfulness and Stress Reduction

Subsection 8.1: Incorporating Mindfulness Practices
Mindfulness practices, such as meditation and deep breathing, contribute to resilience by promoting self-awareness and reducing stress. Integrating these practices into daily routines enhances mental fortitude.

Subsection 8.2: Stress Reduction Techniques

Developing stress reduction techniques, including time management, prioritization, and setting realistic goals, empowers individuals to navigate challenges without succumbing to overwhelming stress.

Section 9: Building a Supportive Network

Subsection 9.1: The Importance of Social Support
Social support is a cornerstone of resilience. Cultivating a supportive network of friends, family, and colleagues creates a safety net during challenging times, fostering emotional well-being.

Subsection 9.2: Seeking Professional Support
In times of significant adversity, seeking professional support from therapists, counselors, or mentors can be instrumental. Professional guidance provides individuals with tools and strategies to enhance resilience.

Learning from Adversity:

Section 10: Extracting Growth from Challenges

Subsection 10.1: The Concept of Post-Traumatic Growth
Post-traumatic growth involves extracting positive outcomes from adversity. Resilient individuals leverage challenges as opportunities for self-discovery, personal development, and the cultivation of newfound strengths.

Subsection 10.2: Learning Resilience from Role Models
Role models who have demonstrated resilience serve as inspirational figures. Examining their journeys, understanding how they navigated challenges, and applying those lessons contribute to personal resilience.

Resilience Case Studies:

Section 11: Inspirational Narratives

Subsection 11.1: [Name] - Rising from Personal Adversity
Explore the inspirational story of [Name], who rose from personal adversity through resilience and determination. [Name]'s narrative highlights the transformative power of facing challenges with courage.

Subsection 11.2: [Another Name] - Career Resilience in the Face of Setbacks
Learn from the experiences of [Another Name], who navigated career setbacks with resilience. [Another Name]'s story provides insights into overcoming professional challenges and emerging stronger.

Teaching Resilience to the Next Generation:

Section 12: Fostering Resilience in Children

Subsection 12.1: The Role of Parenting in Building Resilience
Parenting plays a pivotal role in fostering resilience in children. Encouraging independence, teaching problem-solving skills, and providing emotional support contribute to a child's ability to bounce back from adversity.

Subsection 12.2: Educational Initiatives for Resilience
Educational institutions can play a part in teaching resilience. Implementing programs that focus on emotional intelligence, coping strategies, and character development equips students with essential life skills.

Future Challenges and Resilience:

Section 13: Adapting to Technological and Social Changes

Subsection 13.1: Resilience in the Digital Age

The digital age presents unique challenges that require resilience. Adapting to technological advancements, navigating online interactions, and maintaining mental health in a connected world are crucial aspects of contemporary resilience.

Subsection 13.2: Addressing Global Challenges
Global challenges, such as climate change and socio-economic shifts, necessitate a collective and resilient response. Individuals and communities that prioritize adaptability and collaboration are better positioned to address these challenges.

Conclusion:

In conclusion, overcoming challenges and cultivating resilience is an ongoing journey that encompasses personal, professional, and societal dimensions. By understanding the adaptive nature of resilience, implementing strategies for mental fortitude, and learning from adversity, individuals can navigate life's uncertainties and emerge stronger. Resilience is not just about bouncing back; it's about bouncing forward, equipped with newfound strength, wisdom, and a resilient mindset that propels individuals towards continued growth and success.

Chapter 15: Embracing Technology - The Driver of Future Wealth

In an era characterized by rapid technological advancements, embracing technology has become synonymous with unlocking unparalleled opportunities for wealth creation. This chapter delves into the transformative power of technology, exploring its role as a catalyst for innovation, entrepreneurship, and sustained financial prosperity.

The Evolution of Technology:

Section 1: A Historical Perspective

Subsection 1.1: From Industrial Revolutions to Digital Transformation
Examining the historical trajectory of technological evolution, from the Industrial Revolutions to the current era of digital transformation, lays the foundation for understanding the profound impact technology has had on wealth creation.

Subsection 1.2: Accelerating Pace of Innovation

The pace of technological innovation continues to accelerate, ushering in unprecedented possibilities. Exploring key milestones and breakthroughs provides insights into the dynamic landscape shaping the future of wealth.

The Digital Economy:

Section 2: Shifting Paradigms

Subsection 2.1: The Rise of the Digital Economy

The digital economy has emerged as a dominant force, reshaping industries and redefining the nature of wealth creation. Understanding the dynamics of this shift is essential for individuals seeking to navigate and thrive in the digital landscape.

Subsection 2.2: Opportunities in E-Commerce and Online Markets

E-commerce and online markets represent thriving sectors within the digital economy. Exploring opportunities for entrepreneurship, investment, and innovation in these realms unveils avenues for future wealth accumulation.

Technological Entrepreneurship:

Section 3: Fostering Innovation

Subsection 3.1: Entrepreneurial Opportunities in Tech Startups

Tech startups have become hotbeds of innovation, disrupting traditional industries and creating new market spaces. Examining the entrepreneurial landscape in technology unveils strategies for wealth creation through innovation.

Subsection 3.2: Navigating Funding Ecosystems

Access to funding is crucial for tech entrepreneurs. Exploring diverse funding sources, from venture capital to crowdfunding, provides insights into navigating the financial ecosystem and fueling technological ventures.

Investing in Technological Assets:

Section 4: Wealth Generation through Investments

Subsection 4.1: The Power of Tech Investments
Investing in technological assets, from stocks to cryptocurrencies, has emerged as a potent strategy for wealth generation. Analyzing investment opportunities in the tech sector guides individuals towards informed and strategic financial decisions.

Subsection 4.2: Risk Management in Tech Investments
While technology investments offer immense potential, effective risk management is paramount. Understanding the risks associated with tech investments and implementing strategies to mitigate them safeguard financial portfolios.

Leveraging Artificial Intelligence:

Section 5: The AI Revolution

Subsection 5.1: Transformative Impact of Artificial Intelligence
Artificial Intelligence (AI) stands at the forefront of technological advancements, revolutionizing industries and creating efficiencies. Exploring the transformative impact of AI provides a roadmap for leveraging this technology for wealth creation.

Subsection 5.2: AI in Business and Entrepreneurship
Integrating AI into business strategies and entrepreneurial endeavors unlocks unprecedented opportunities. Examining case studies and success stories illustrates how AI can be harnessed as a strategic tool for wealth accumulation.

Digital Marketing Strategies:

Section 6: Navigating the Online Marketplace

Subsection 6.1: The Role of Digital Marketing
Digital marketing has become a cornerstone for success in the online marketplace. Understanding effective digital marketing strategies empowers entrepreneurs and businesses to thrive in the digital economy.

Subsection 6.2: Building an Online Presence
Establishing a robust online presence is crucial for individuals and businesses alike. Exploring techniques for effective branding, social media engagement, and content marketing lays the groundwork for sustained visibility and success.

E-Learning and Skill Development:

Section 7: Knowledge as a Currency

Subsection 7.1: The E-Learning Revolution
E-learning has democratized access to knowledge, making education a key driver of future wealth. Exploring the role of online education in skill development and continuous learning unveils pathways for personal and professional growth.

Subsection 7.2: Skill Sets for the Digital Age
Identifying and cultivating skill sets relevant to the digital age is imperative. Analyzing the in-demand skills across industries guides individuals towards acquiring competencies that enhance employability and entrepreneurial success.

Blockchain and Decentralization:

Section 8: The Decentralized Future

Subsection 8.1: Blockchain Technology Unveiled

Blockchain technology, underpinning cryptocurrencies, has far-reaching implications beyond finance. Exploring the decentralized nature of blockchain and its potential applications provides insights into future opportunities.

Subsection 8.2: Decentralized Finance (DeFi)

Decentralized Finance, or DeFi, represents a paradigm shift in traditional financial systems. Understanding the principles of DeFi and exploring investment and entrepreneurial opportunities within this space unveils novel avenues for wealth creation.

Sustainability and Green Technologies:

Section 9: Wealth with a Purpose

Subsection 9.1: Green Technologies for Sustainable Wealth

The intersection of technology and sustainability offers opportunities for wealth creation with a purpose. Exploring green technologies and environmentally conscious innovations guides individuals towards investments aligned with global sustainability goals.

Subsection 9.2: Corporate Social Responsibility in the Tech Industry

Tech companies are increasingly embracing Corporate Social Responsibility (CSR) initiatives. Analyzing how tech firms contribute to societal well-being provides insights into aligning wealth creation with social and environmental responsibility.

Cybersecurity and Risk Mitigation:

Section 10: Safeguarding Wealth in the Digital Age

Subsection 10.1: The Critical Role of Cybersecurity

As technology advances, the need for robust cybersecurity measures intensifies. Understanding the importance of cybersecurity in safeguarding wealth and mitigating risks is essential for individuals and businesses operating in the digital landscape.

Subsection 10.2: Insurance Strategies for the Digital Era
In the digital era, insurance strategies must adapt to new challenges. Exploring insurance options and risk mitigation strategies tailored to the tech landscape ensures comprehensive protection of wealth.

The Future of Technology and Wealth:

Section 11: Anticipating Trends and Staying Ahead

Subsection 11.1: Emerging Technologies on the Horizon
Anticipating emerging technologies, from quantum computing to biotechnology, provides a glimpse into the future. Examining these trends enables individuals to position themselves at the forefront of technological advancements for sustained wealth creation.

Subsection 11.2: Continuous Adaptability as a Key Success Factor
In the ever-evolving tech landscape, continuous adaptability is a key success factor. Cultivating a mindset of lifelong learning and adaptability ensures individuals can harness future technologies for ongoing wealth generation.

Ethical Considerations in Technology:

Section 12: Balancing Innovation and Responsibility

Subsection 12.1: Ethical Tech Innovation
As technology progresses, ethical considerations become paramount. Balancing innovation with responsibility ensures that wealth creation aligns with ethical principles, contributing to a sustainable and inclusive future.

Subsection 12.2: Addressing Societal Impacts
Examining the societal impacts of technological advancements, both positive and negative, informs ethical decision-making. Understanding the broader consequences of tech-driven wealth creation guides individuals towards responsible and impactful choices.

Case Studies in Tech-Driven Wealth Creation:

Section 13: Success Stories in the Digital Age

Subsection 13.1: [Name] - Pioneering Disruptive Innovations
Explore the success story of [Name], who pioneered disruptive innovations in the tech sector. [Name]'s journey unveils the strategies and mindset that propelled them to the forefront of wealth creation in the digital age.

Subsection 13.2: [Another Name] - From Start-up to Tech Titan
Learn from the experiences of [Another Name], who navigated the challenges of the startup landscape to become a tech titan. This case study provides insights into scaling a tech business and achieving sustained financial success.

Conclusion:

In conclusion, embracing technology emerges as a transformative pathway to future wealth. From entrepreneurial ventures and tech investments to the ethical considerations shaping innovation, this chapter navigates the multifaceted landscape of technology-driven wealth creation. As individuals embrace the opportunities presented by the digital era, cultivating a proactive and adaptable approach ensures not only financial prosperity but also a meaningful contribution to the evolving tapestry of technological innovation and societal progress.

Chapter 16: Global Opportunities - Expanding Your Financial Horizons

In an interconnected world, the pursuit of financial success extends beyond local borders. This chapter explores the vast landscape of global opportunities, providing insights into international investments, cross-border entrepreneurship, and strategies for expanding financial horizons on a global scale.

Understanding the Global Economy:

Section 1: Navigating the International Marketplace

Subsection 1.1: The Dynamics of the Global Economy
Understanding the interconnectedness of the global economy is fundamental. Exploring economic trends, trade dynamics, and the role of emerging markets sets the stage for individuals seeking to tap into global opportunities.

Subsection 1.2: Impact of Global Events on Financial Markets

Global events, from geopolitical shifts to pandemics, can have profound effects on financial markets. Analyzing the impact of these events equips individuals with the knowledge to navigate and capitalize on dynamic global conditions.

International Investments:

Section 2: Diversifying Your Investment Portfolio

Subsection 2.1: Opportunities in Global Stock Markets
Diversifying investments across global stock markets provides exposure to diverse industries and economic cycles. Understanding the intricacies of international stock markets guides individuals in building a resilient and globally diversified portfolio.

Subsection 2.2: Exploring Foreign Exchange (Forex) Markets
Foreign exchange markets offer opportunities for currency trading and hedging. Delving into the dynamics of Forex markets equips individuals with tools to navigate currency fluctuations and capitalize on global economic trends.

Real Estate on a Global Scale:

Section 3: Global Property Investment Strategies

Subsection 3.1: Investing in International Real Estate
International real estate investment presents opportunities for portfolio diversification and potential high returns. Examining strategies for investing in global properties, from residential to commercial assets, provides a roadmap for success.

Subsection 3.2: Navigating Real Estate Regulations Worldwide
Real estate regulations vary across countries. Understanding the legal and regulatory frameworks in different regions is crucial for making informed decisions and mitigating risks in global property investments.

Cross-Border Entrepreneurship:

Section 4: Entrepreneurial Ventures Beyond Borders

Subsection 4.1: Identifying Global Market Gaps
Entrepreneurs can identify market gaps and untapped opportunities on a global scale. Analyzing consumer needs, cultural nuances, and regulatory environments assists in crafting successful cross-border entrepreneurial ventures.

Subsection 4.2: Overcoming Challenges in Global Business
Operating a business across borders comes with challenges. From navigating cultural differences to managing logistics, exploring strategies for overcoming these challenges ensures the resilience and success of global entrepreneurial endeavors.

International Trade and Import-Export:

Section 5: Harnessing the Power of Global Trade

Subsection 5.1: Opportunities in Import-Export Businesses
Participating in import-export businesses opens doors to global trade opportunities. Understanding trade regulations, logistics, and market trends is essential for individuals looking to venture into this dynamic arena.

Subsection 5.2: Utilizing Free Trade Agreements
Free trade agreements facilitate smoother international trade. Examining the impact of free trade agreements and understanding how to leverage them enhances the efficiency and profitability of global trade ventures.

Digital Nomadism and Remote Work:

Section 6: Embracing Location Independence

Subsection 6.1: Digital Nomad Lifestyle

The rise of digital nomadism allows individuals to work from anywhere in the world. Exploring the digital nomad lifestyle, from choosing remote work destinations to managing work-life balance, unveils opportunities for a global career.

Subsection 6.2: Remote Work Strategies for Employers

Employers can tap into global talent pools by embracing remote work. Implementing effective remote work strategies, including virtual collaboration tools and flexible policies, contributes to a global and diverse workforce.

Global Networking and Collaboration:

Section 7: Building a Global Professional Network

Subsection 7.1: Leveraging International Networking Platforms

International networking platforms connect professionals across borders. Understanding how to leverage these platforms for collaboration, mentorship, and business opportunities expands the scope of global professional networks.

Subsection 7.2: Cross-Cultural Communication Skills

Effective cross-cultural communication is crucial in global business. Developing cultural intelligence, language skills, and awareness of cultural nuances enhances interpersonal relationships and fosters successful collaborations worldwide.

Educational Opportunities Worldwide:

Section 8: Pursuing Global Education and Skills

Subsection 8.1: Studying Abroad for Career Advancement

Studying abroad opens doors to global educational opportunities. Exploring the benefits of international education and strategies for leveraging global academic experiences enhances career prospects and personal growth.

Subsection 8.2: Online Learning Platforms for Global Skill Enhancement
Online learning platforms provide accessible opportunities for global skill enhancement. Identifying reputable platforms, navigating diverse course offerings, and acquiring globally relevant skills contribute to professional development.

Philanthropy on a Global Scale:

Section 9: Making a Global Impact

Subsection 9.1: Global Philanthropy and Social Impact
Philanthropy can extend beyond local communities to address global challenges. Exploring avenues for global philanthropy, from supporting international charities to funding sustainable development projects, allows individuals to make a positive impact on a global scale.

Subsection 9.2: Corporate Social Responsibility in Global Business
Businesses can contribute to global social responsibility. Examining successful corporate social responsibility (CSR) initiatives on a global scale highlights the role of businesses in addressing societal challenges and fostering sustainable development.

Legal and Regulatory Considerations:

Section 10: Navigating Global Legal Frameworks

Subsection 10.1: Understanding International Business Laws
International business involves navigating diverse legal frameworks. Understanding international business laws, trade agreements, and compliance requirements ensures individuals and businesses operate within legal boundaries.

Subsection 10.2: Legal Considerations for Global Investments
Investing globally requires attention to legal considerations. Examining taxation, property laws, and investment regulations in different countries empowers individuals to make informed decisions and protect their financial interests.

Cultural Intelligence for Global Success:

Section 11: Cultivating Cultural Intelligence

Subsection 11.1: The Importance of Cultural Intelligence
Cultural intelligence is a key asset for success in global endeavors. Developing cultural sensitivity, adaptability, and interpersonal skills fosters effective communication and collaboration across diverse cultural contexts.

Subsection 11.2: Cultural Awareness in Marketing and Business
Cultural awareness plays a pivotal role in global marketing and business strategies. Tailoring marketing campaigns, products, and services to align with diverse cultural preferences enhances the success of global business initiatives.

Risk Management in Global Ventures:

Section 12: Mitigating Risks Across Borders

Subsection 12.1: Identifying and Assessing Global Risks
Operating globally involves navigating a range of risks, from geopolitical uncertainties to currency fluctuations. Identifying and assessing these risks is essential for implementing effective risk management strategies.

Subsection 12.2: Insurance and Legal Safeguards

Insurance and legal safeguards are crucial components of risk mitigation in global ventures. Understanding the types of insurance and legal protections available, and tailoring them to specific global operations, safeguards financial interests.

Sustainable Global Business Practices:

Section 13: Sustainability in a Global Context

Subsection 13.1: Global Environmental and Social Responsibility
Global businesses have a role in promoting environmental and social responsibility. Examining sustainable business practices, from reducing carbon footprints to promoting fair labor practices, aligns global ventures with broader sustainability goals.

Subsection 13.2: Ethical Supply Chains in Global Operations
Ensuring ethical supply chains is imperative for global businesses. Evaluating supply chain practices, addressing issues of transparency and accountability, and promoting ethical sourcing contribute to responsible global business operations.

Case Studies in Global Success:

Section 14: Inspirational Global Journeys

Subsection 14.1: [Name] - Building a Global Business Empire
Explore the success story of [Name], who built a global business empire. [Name]'s journey highlights strategies for international expansion, overcoming challenges, and achieving sustained success on a global scale.

Subsection 14.2: [Another Name] - Philanthropic Endeavors Across Continents
Learn from the experiences of [Another Name], who engaged in philanthropic endeavors across continents. This case study illustrates the impact of global philanthropy and how individuals can contribute to positive change on a global scale.

Future Trends in Global Opportunities:

Section 15: Anticipating the Global Landscape

Subsection 15.1: Emerging Markets and Industries
Anticipating emerging markets and industries on a global scale provides foresight into future opportunities. Examining trends in technology, renewable energy, and healthcare unveils potential areas for global investment and entrepreneurship.

Subsection 15.2: Global Megatrends Shaping the Future
Global megatrends, from demographic shifts to technological advancements, shape the future landscape. Understanding these megatrends positions individuals to proactively navigate global opportunities and align financial strategies with future realities.

Conclusion:

In conclusion, expanding financial horizons on a global scale opens doors to a myriad of opportunities. From international investments and cross-border entrepreneurship to embracing a global mindset, this chapter provides a comprehensive guide for individuals seeking to thrive in the interconnected world of global opportunities. By understanding the nuances of global dynamics, mitigating risks, and embracing sustainable and ethical practices, individuals can embark on a journey of financial success that transcends geographical boundaries and contributes to a more inclusive and interconnected global economy.

Chapter 17: FAQs - Answering the Top 30 Questions About Financial Freedom

Financial freedom is a pursuit that involves navigating a complex landscape of personal finance, career choices, and investment strategies. This chapter addresses the most pressing questions individuals often have about achieving financial freedom. From understanding the basics to tackling more nuanced inquiries, here are detailed responses to the top 30 questions.

1. What is Financial Freedom?

Financial freedom is a state where an individual has sufficient financial resources to cover their living expenses and pursue their desired lifestyle without being constrained by the need to work for a paycheck. It involves creating a financial situation that provides independence and the ability to make choices based on personal preferences rather than financial necessity.

2. How Can I Determine My Financial Goals?

Determining financial goals involves assessing both short-term and long-term objectives. Start by identifying specific goals such as buying a home, funding education, or retiring comfortably. Quantify these goals, set timelines, and prioritize them based on importance. Regularly review and adjust your goals as your financial situation evolves.

3. Is It Better to Save or Invest?

Saving and investing serve different purposes. Saving is for short-term goals and emergencies, typically kept in accessible accounts. Investing, on the other hand, involves putting money into assets with the expectation of generating returns over the long term. A balanced approach involves both saving for immediate needs and investing for future growth.

4. What are the Key Principles of Smart Investing?

Smart investing involves understanding risk, diversification, and having a long-term perspective. Diversify your investments across different assets to mitigate risk. Stay informed about market trends but avoid making impulsive decisions based on short-term fluctuations. Additionally, consider seeking professional advice to make informed investment choices.

5. How Can I Create a Budget for Financial Success?

Creating a budget is foundational for financial success. Start by listing your income sources and categorize your expenses. Differentiate between essential and discretionary spending. Allocate a portion of your income to savings and investments. Regularly review and adjust your budget to align with your financial goals.

6. What is the Importance of Emergency Funds?

Emergency funds are a financial safety net. They provide a cushion for unexpected expenses such as medical emergencies or job loss, preventing you from dipping into long-term investments or going into debt. Aim to build an emergency fund that covers three to six months' worth of living expenses.

7. How Can I Pay Off Debt Strategically?

Strategic debt repayment involves prioritizing high-interest debts and using methods like the debt snowball or debt avalanche. The debt snowball focuses on paying off the smallest debts first, while the debt avalanche tackles high-interest debts to minimize overall interest payments. Consistency and discipline are key to successful debt repayment.

8. Should I Prioritize Saving for Retirement or Other Goals?

Balancing retirement savings with other financial goals depends on your individual circumstances. Generally, it's advisable to prioritize retirement savings due to the power of compounding over time. However, finding a balance that allows you to address immediate goals while still contributing to retirement accounts is crucial for holistic financial planning.

9. How Can I Maximize Tax Efficiency in Investments?

Maximizing tax efficiency involves understanding tax-advantaged accounts such as IRAs and 401(k)s, where contributions may be tax-deductible or grow tax-deferred. Additionally, consider tax-efficient investment strategies, like holding investments for the long term to benefit from lower capital gains tax rates.

10. Is Real Estate a Good Investment?

Real estate can be a viable investment, offering potential appreciation and rental income. However, it comes with risks and requires careful research. Factors such as location, market trends, and property management play crucial roles. Diversifying investments, including real estate, can contribute to a well-rounded portfolio.

11. What Role Does Education Play in Financial Success?

Education is a powerful tool for financial success. Continuously invest in your financial literacy to make informed decisions about budgeting, investing, and managing debt. Additionally, acquiring skills through education enhances employability, career growth, and potential income.

12. How Can I Negotiate a Salary Raise?

Negotiating a salary raise involves preparation and confidence. Research industry salary benchmarks, highlight your accomplishments, and be ready to articulate the value you bring to the organization. Practice effective communication, and approach the negotiation with a collaborative mindset.

13. What's the Significance of Networking in Career Growth?

Networking is integral to career growth. Building professional relationships opens doors to opportunities, mentorship, and industry insights. Attend industry events, engage on professional platforms, and cultivate meaningful connections. A strong professional network enhances visibility and can lead to career advancements.

14. How Can I Start a Side Business for Extra Income?

Starting a side business involves identifying your skills and interests. Evaluate market demands and potential profitability. Create a business plan, establish a digital presence, and leverage online platforms for marketing. Ensure legal compliance and start small, gradually scaling as your business gains traction.

15. Is Passive Income Achievable, and How Can I Generate It?

Passive income is attainable through investments, real estate, or creating digital assets. Common sources include dividends from stocks, rental income from real estate, or income generated from online businesses. Building passive income requires initial effort but can provide financial freedom over time.

16. What Retirement Planning Strategies Should I Consider?

Retirement planning involves assessing your retirement needs, setting goals, and choosing appropriate investment vehicles. Contribute consistently to retirement accounts, take advantage of employer-sponsored plans, and consider diversifying investments to balance risk and return.

17. How Can I Navigate Market Volatility in Investments?

Market volatility is inevitable, and navigating it requires a disciplined approach. Stay focused on long-term goals, avoid reacting emotionally to short-term fluctuations, and consider periodic rebalancing of your portfolio. Diversification and maintaining a diversified asset allocation help mitigate the impact of market volatility.

18. Can I Achieve Financial Freedom through Frugality?

Frugality is a valuable tool for achieving financial freedom. It involves mindful spending, prioritizing needs over wants, and seeking cost-effective alternatives. By adopting a frugal lifestyle, you can increase savings, reduce debt, and accelerate progress toward financial goals.

19. How Can I Ensure Financial Success for the Next Generation?

Ensuring financial success for the next generation involves education and estate planning. Instill financial literacy in your children, involve them in financial discussions, and set up savings or investment accounts for their future. Establishing a well-thought-out estate plan ensures a smooth transfer of assets.

20. What Strategies Can I Use to Protect My Investments?

Protecting investments involves diversification, staying informed, and having a risk management strategy. Diversify across asset classes and industries to spread risk. Stay updated on market trends, and consider using tools like stop-loss orders for active risk management.

21. How Can I Balance Investing for Growth and Income?

Balancing growth and income involves diversifying investments across growth-oriented and income-generating assets. Growth assets, like stocks, offer potential capital appreciation, while income assets, such as bonds or dividend-paying stocks, provide regular cash flow. Finding the right mix aligns with individual financial goals and risk tolerance.

22. What Steps Should I Take Before Starting a Business?

Before starting a business, conduct thorough market research to understand demand and competition. Create a comprehensive business plan outlining your goals, target audience, and financial projections. Address legal requirements, secure necessary permits, and establish a strong digital presence.

23. How Can I Navigate Economic Recessions for Financial Security?

Navigating economic recessions involves prudent financial management. Build an emergency fund, reduce discretionary spending, and prioritize debt repayment. Diversify investments to mitigate risk and consider opportunities that may arise in undervalued markets.

24. Can I Achieve Financial Freedom Through Investments Alone?

While investments play a crucial role in financial freedom, a holistic approach is essential. Combine smart investing with budgeting, debt management, and strategic career choices. Consider additional income streams, such as side businesses or passive income, to enhance financial stability.

25. How Can I Make Informed Investment Decisions?

Making informed investment decisions requires research and staying informed. Understand the fundamentals of the investments you're considering, assess risk tolerance, and diversify your portfolio. Stay updated on market trends, economic indicators, and seek advice from financial professionals when needed.

26. Should I Pay Off Mortgage Early or Invest?

The decision to pay off a mortgage early or invest depends on individual preferences and financial goals. Compare the interest rate on the mortgage with potential investment returns. If the mortgage rate is low, investing may yield higher returns. If debt reduction is a priority, paying off the mortgage early provides peace of mind.

27. How Can I Leverage Technology for Financial Management?

Technology offers tools for effective financial management. Utilize budgeting apps, investment platforms, and online banking for streamlined financial tracking. Explore robo-advisors for automated investment management and stay informed about financial news through reputable online sources.

28. Is Early Retirement Feasible, and How Can I Achieve It?

Early retirement is feasible with careful planning. Determine your retirement needs, maximize contributions to retirement accounts, and consider additional savings or investments. Assess healthcare and lifestyle considerations for early retirement and regularly review and adjust your plan.

29. What Role Does Mindset Play in Financial Success?

Mindset plays a significant role in financial success. Cultivate a positive and disciplined mindset, embrace a growth mindset that welcomes learning and adaptation, and avoid limiting beliefs about money. A proactive and optimistic mindset enhances resilience in the face of financial challenges.

30. How Can I Leave a Financial Legacy?

Leaving a financial legacy involves estate planning and thoughtful wealth transfer strategies. Work with professionals to create a comprehensive estate plan, including wills, trusts, and beneficiary designations. Consider philanthropic endeavors or educational funds to contribute positively to future generations.

Conclusion:

In conclusion, achieving financial freedom is a journey that requires a combination of financial literacy, strategic planning, and disciplined execution. By addressing these top 30 questions, individuals can gain a comprehensive understanding of the key principles and practices that contribute to long-term financial success. Remember, financial freedom is not a destination but a continual process of learning, adapting, and making informed decisions to secure a prosperous future.

Chapter 18: Eternal Wealth - A Holistic Approach to Sustainable Prosperity

In the pursuit of financial freedom, the concept of eternal wealth transcends mere accumulation of riches; it encompasses a holistic and sustainable approach to prosperity that extends beyond one's lifetime. This chapter delves into the multifaceted elements of eternal wealth, exploring not only financial aspects but also the enduring legacy individuals can create for themselves and future generations.

The Foundations of Eternal Wealth:

Section 1: Beyond Financial Riches

Subsection 1.1: Defining Eternal Wealth

Eternal wealth goes beyond financial abundance. It encapsulates a wealth of experiences, relationships, knowledge, and positive contributions to society. This broader perspective forms the foundation for a truly enduring legacy.

Subsection 1.2: The Role of Financial Literacy in Eternal Wealth
Financial literacy is a cornerstone of eternal wealth. Understanding how to manage, invest, and grow wealth is essential, enabling individuals to make informed decisions that align with their long-term goals.

Building a Lasting Legacy:

Section 2: Creating a Legacy of Impact

Subsection 2.1: The Power of Purpose
A purpose-driven life contributes to eternal wealth. Discovering and aligning one's actions with a meaningful purpose not only brings personal fulfillment but also leaves a lasting impact on the world.

Subsection 2.2: Philanthropy and Social Responsibility
Contributing to societal well-being ensures a legacy of positive change. Exploring philanthropic endeavors and integrating social responsibility into financial planning amplifies the impact of one's wealth on future generations.

Family and Generational Wealth:

Section 3: Nurturing Generational Prosperity

Subsection 3.1: Financial Education for Successors
Educating future generations about financial principles empowers them to carry the torch of wealth responsibly. Explore strategies for instilling financial literacy in heirs and preparing them for managing inherited wealth.

Subsection 3.2: Estate Planning for Seamless Wealth Transfer

Effective estate planning ensures a smooth transfer of wealth to heirs. Delve into the intricacies of wills, trusts, and inheritance strategies to preserve and grow family wealth across generations.

Sustainable Investments:

Section 4: Investing for the Long-Term

Subsection 4.1: Environmental, Social, and Governance (ESG) Investing

Eternal wealth involves considering the broader impact of investments. Explore ESG investing, aligning financial goals with environmental and social responsibility to create a sustainable and prosperous future.

Subsection 4.2: Impact Investing for Positive Change

Impact investing directs capital toward businesses and projects that generate positive social and environmental outcomes. Discover how integrating impact investments into portfolios can contribute to eternal wealth.

Health and Well-Being:

Section 5: Nurturing the Wealth Within

Subsection 5.1: Investing in Health and Wellness

True wealth encompasses well-being. Explore strategies for investing in physical and mental health, ensuring individuals can enjoy the fruits of their labor and contribute actively to their communities.

Subsection 5.2: Balancing Work and Life for Lasting Fulfillment

Achieving eternal wealth involves striking a balance between professional success and personal fulfillment. Uncover techniques for harmonizing work and life to sustain happiness and well-being.

Cultural and Educational Contributions:

Section 6: Fostering Intellectual and Cultural Riches

Subsection 6.1: Supporting Education and Lifelong Learning

Eternal wealth involves the continuous pursuit of knowledge. Discover the significance of supporting educational initiatives and fostering a culture of lifelong learning within families and communities.

Subsection 6.2: Patronage of the Arts and Culture

Contributing to the arts and cultural endeavors enriches the human experience. Explore how individuals can become patrons, supporting creativity and preserving cultural heritage for generations to come.

Technology and Innovation for Posterity:

Section 7: Embracing Technological Advancements

Subsection 7.1: Future-Proofing Through Technology

Eternal wealth requires embracing technological advancements. Explore how staying abreast of technological trends and innovations ensures adaptability and relevance in a rapidly evolving world.

Subsection 7.2: Tech Philanthropy - Catalyzing Positive Change

The tech sector presents opportunities for philanthropy. Examine how tech leaders can contribute to societal well-being, leveraging their resources and influence for lasting positive change.

Wisdom from Successful Stewards of Eternal Wealth:

Section 8: Case Studies in Eternal Wealth

Subsection 8.1: [Name] - A Legacy of Innovation and Social Impact

Explore the life and contributions of [Name], an individual who forged an eternal legacy through innovation and impactful social initiatives. Uncover the lessons learned and strategies employed for sustainable prosperity.

Subsection 8.2: [Another Name] - Preserving Cultural Heritage Through Generations
Learn from the experiences of [Another Name], a steward of cultural heritage. Understand the approaches taken to preserve and pass down cultural richness, ensuring a vibrant legacy for future generations.

Future-Proofing Against Economic Challenges:

Section 9: Strategies for Financial Resilience

Subsection 9.1: Building Resilient Wealth Structures
Eternal wealth requires resilience against economic uncertainties. Explore strategies for building robust financial structures that can weather economic downturns and ensure the continuity of prosperity.

Subsection 9.2: Adaptive Strategies for Changing Economic Landscapes
Adaptability is key to enduring wealth. Delve into adaptive strategies that individuals and families can employ to navigate changing economic landscapes and emerge stronger.

Environmental Stewardship:

Section 10: Sustaining Wealth Through Eco-Conscious Practices

Subsection 10.1: Green Investments for a Sustainable Future
Eternal wealth intertwines with environmental sustainability. Explore green investment opportunities that contribute to both financial growth and a sustainable planet.

Subsection 10.2: Eco-Friendly Estate Planning and Property Management
Incorporating eco-friendly practices into estate planning and property management aligns with the principles of eternal wealth. Discover how sustainable choices can contribute to a lasting and harmonious environment.

The Spiritual Dimension of Eternal Wealth:

Section 11: Inner Prosperity and Fulfillment

Subsection 11.1: Exploring Spiritual Wealth
Beyond the material realm, eternal wealth encompasses spiritual fulfillment. Uncover the significance of cultivating inner peace, gratitude, and a sense of purpose as integral components of enduring prosperity.

Subsection 11.2: Mindfulness and Wealth Management
Mindfulness practices play a role in wealth management. Explore how incorporating mindfulness into financial decisions enhances clarity, reduces stress, and contributes to a more balanced approach to wealth.

Conclusion:

In conclusion, eternal wealth is a grand tapestry woven from diverse threads of financial wisdom, impactful contributions, cultural preservation, and a deep commitment to holistic well-being. This chapter serves as a guide for individuals aspiring to leave a lasting legacy—one that transcends generations, enriches communities, and stands as a testament to a life well-lived. By embracing a comprehensive approach to wealth, individuals can not only accumulate financial riches but also sow the seeds of prosperity that endure for eternity.